The Author's Guide

to

PLANNING

BOOK EVENTS

The Author's Guide

to

PLANNING
BOOK EVENTS

Tips and Tools for Bookselling Success

CAROL HOENIG

Author of the Award-Winning Novel
Without Grace

iUniverse Star
New York   Lincoln   Shanghai

The Author's Guide to PLANNING BOOK EVENTS
Tips and Tools for Bookselling Success

iUniverse Star
an iUniverse, Inc. imprint

iUniverse books may be ordered through booksellers or by contacting:

iUniverse
2021 Pine Lake Road, Suite 100
Lincoln, NE 68512
www.iuniverse.com
1-800-Authors (1-800-288-4677)

Because of the dynamic nature of the Internet, any Web addresses
or links contained in this book may have changed
since publication and may no longer be valid.

The views expressed in this work are solely those of the author and do not necessarily reflect the views of the publisher, and the publisher hereby disclaims any responsibility for them.

ISBN: 978-1-58348-476-0 (pbk)
ISBN: 978-0-595-88353-0 (ebk)

Printed in the United States of America

CONTENTS

Part 2: You Have a Due Date! 29

ACKNOWLEDGMENTS

There are hundreds of people whom I want to thank; however, I will take the risk of naming just a few here.

First, I must thank Susan Driscoll, CEO of iUniverse, who has given me the opportunity to share what I've learned from my experiences via this book. I will always be grateful for her constant support and encouragement.

P. J. Campbell has shown me the difference between trying and succeeding. Thank you, PJ, for your uplifting words and encouraging e-mails. Thanks, too, for photographing my book launch for *Without Grace*. I will always value our friendship.

Cathy, Gloria, Nick, Lisa, and Chuck, while I was creating a world within narrative dimensions, you were constructing a solid one from sheetrock, flooring, and gallons of paint—for me. Thank you for allowing me the freedom to flesh out a novel while you built me a house from the ground up. It is mind-boggling, but so very much appreciated.

No matter how assertive an author is in getting their book into the hands of readers, without the support and encouragement of so many, the task would be impossible. There are many readers, publicists, interviewers, and good friends who have tirelessly promoted my works, but there are a select few booksellers, due to their diligence and great persistence in helping me reach my audience, that I must thank here:

Peggy Zieran, bookselling guru and great friend, not to mention someone willing to travel all along the Eastern Seaboard with me to promote my novel *Without Grace*, has supported my career goals without question. Peggy photographed many of the pictures in this book. Sometimes no matter how eloquent the words are, they cannot express the gratefulness one feels for such encouragement. Peggy, thank you for keeping it real and for helping me in my endeavors. Thanks, too, goes to Peggy's staff, who have consistently sold and recommended my novel to their customers while helping me in reaching a wider audience. At the risk of omitting someone, I personally want to thank Jenielle Bailey, Kristen Capria, Mike Christiansen, Natasha Dasani, Dorothy Fitch, Michele Gaffner, Will Kowalchuk, Stacey Ledovsky, Mary Grace Molluso, Eric Rosenberg, Chris Seifering, and Diane Sinnott, who have introduced me to countless readers, which is what I call a very powerful ripple effect. Thanks one and all for believing in me and helping me on my career path.

Finally, thanks to everyone who took the time to let me interview him or her for this book. Authors seeking to do events will gain valuable information because of your generous advice. I wish every author the friendship that I have experienced on this journey.

FOREWORD

Here is what some have said about Carol:

Carol Hoenig brings to her book the same thing she brings to every event she plans—a savvy mix of business and pleasure that gets results! —Carmine DeSena, award-winning nonfiction and humor writer whose work has been seen and heard in the *New York Times*, *Us* magazine, *Modern Maturity*, and the ABC radio networks. He has published five books, including the highly acclaimed *The Air Down Here: True Tales of a Bronx Boyhood.*

Carol is very gifted in planning and coordinating events and knows how to produce results. She knows what it takes to promote a book and provides this valuable information in this one. Anyone who has a book will benefit from reading Carol's instructional guide on how to promote it.—Agapi Stassinopoulos, author of *Conversations with the Goddesses* and *Gods and Goddesses in Love*

Carol is the perfect mix of what you look for in an event planner: she is knowledgeable, accessible, and attentive. She knows her audience as well as the resources at her command; shake (not stir) liberally with some outside-the-box thinking, and you have the makings for a near-perfect event. We wish we could place her on our payroll.—Kim and Danny Adlerman, authors, illustrator, and musician

I very much enjoyed your talk; you are my role model for small press success!—Cindy Gallagher, author of *Far Above Rubies,* using the pen name Cynthia Polansky

Excellent workshop at BookExpo of America. You gave so much wonderful information; I can't wait to go through all of my notes. I learned so much.—Janet Spurr, author

It was great meeting you and participating in your interesting seminar at the recent BookExpo in Washington DC. I wish it were a weekend seminar with you, instead of only an hour. Ray Seager, my business associate, and I walked away from your seminar in Washington DC saying, "It was the most informative session of the entire Expo." You're terrific, Carol! Love your ideas, your energy, your knowledge, experience, creativity, and sensitivity. It all works!—Barbara Valentine, author of *Who Really Gives A Rat's Ass!*

INTRODUCTION

You've labored for hours writing your book, and now it's about to be published. Congratulations! But the work is far from over. As a matter of fact, it is really just beginning, especially if you want your book to rise above the competition. Chances are, you have either attended or heard about an author event where the line wrapped around the building. However, unless you are already a celebrity with a fan base, you have your work cut out for you in order to get even a small gathering. But don't be discouraged. Even some better-known authors have a difficult time getting a crowd to attend their events for any number of reasons. This book will help you avoid the mistakes that many authors make while simultaneously empowering you with information that will help you save time and money and give you a leg up over all the other books seeking attention out there in the vast world of publishing. You will discover the variety of ways you can bring together a crowd, as well as how to get them to want to buy your book, from someone who has worked as an events coordinator for a major bookstore chain, first locally and then nationally, for over eleven years, as well as a published author of an award-winning novel.

That would be me.

I've worked with a variety of publishers, from independent to traditional ones. I've also booked events for authors who were just getting started and those who'd been doing events for years and are household names. I worked with Suze Orman for her first book, well before she had her own television show, and I've booked signings for former President Jimmy Carter—not once, but twice.

I have also been my own marketing guru, promoting my novel, *Without Grace* (iUniverse Star), for over a year, and still going strong thanks to receiving the Silver Medal for Book of the Year from *ForeWord* magazine and first place for fiction from DIY Book Festival. Of course, like most authors, I cannot survive solely on my writing, so I also am a freelance publishing consultant and editor.

Not only will you read about my experiences in the publishing world, you will also read advice from other authors, publicists, and editors. Since I have been able to participate as both an author and events coordinator, I have an advantage of seeing what works and what doesn't, and I will share the reasons why. While you are reading the many examples provided, think about how they may apply to your own book. But, you say, you haven't finished writing your book yet. I say, all the better! This will give you time to create a strategy and find your audience. Keep a notebook handy, jot down any possible ideas for yourself, and be prepared to implement them.

Now, let's begin.

Part 1

BEFORE YOU PUBLISH

Chapter 1

CREATE A STRATEGY

IT ALL STARTS WITH WHO

It is an exciting time for writers. Now, more than ever, there are a number of ways to get a book into the hands of readers. Let me state right here that a majority of the authors I interviewed for this book are self-published. Besides the fact that they were readily accessible, I thought it would be important for you to see what a self-published author can do in the arena of events and not just those traditionally published, who you may feel have some advantages; namely, distribution. Therefore, whether you will be working with a publicist, one assigned by your publisher or one that you've hired, or doing it on your own, you need to have a strategy. But before we discuss the strategy, you need to understand that even if you do have a publicist, he or she will have other clients' books to promote, so much of the work will fall back onto your shoulders. That's the bad news. The good news is that no one knows your book better than you do. It is your child, so you should already have a strong sense of how to nurture it to success.

TIME TO GESTATE

Even *before* your book has been written, you should have a market or audience in mind. This holds true whether you are writing a historical novel or a book on cryogenics. Over the years, I have attended a large number of writers' conferences where hopeful writers were asked the all-important question: "Who is your audience?" Invariably, the answer would be, "Everyone!" There was the belief that their book was going to be for everyone, in hopes that a publisher would say, "Wow! This will be easy to sell since *everyone* will buy it!"

Unfortunately, that cannot be the case.

Simply walk into any bookstore and you will see that it is divided into categories and subcategories. There is not only a section for fiction, but within that section is mystery, romance, horror, and more. The reason the section is shelved thusly is because the market knows every customer has a preference. It will be the same when it comes to marketing your book. As the author of your book, you will need to spend time reaching out to those who will be interested in what you have to say while avoiding expending energy that will yield no return. So, even before you dot every *i* and cross every *t*, think about who your market is. Figuring out who you market is will save you time and money, and the promotion and planning will be easier.

Therefore, do not attempt to book event space just yet. What you should be doing right now is keeping notes of the contacts you are making at conferences, PTA meetings, and any other social gatherings you attend. Also, continually update your Rolodex or Outlook contacts, and hold on to all those business cards you are managing to acquire. However, let me offer one piece of advice regarding those cards: jot on the back when and where you've met the person whose name is on the card, as well as a significant detail that will jog your memory. This way, when you call or e-mail the contact about an upcoming event you are scheduled to do, you can personalize your message and be impressive enough to make them take notice. While you are updating your contact list, you will get a clearer idea of who your audience will be when writing your book. Quite likely, you are wondering just how that works.

GET INTIMATE WITH YOUR BOOK

As I said, no one knows your book better than you do, but sometimes knowing how to present it clearly is the problem. Therefore, you must begin thinking of yourself as *more* than an author. You are now your own marketing guru. It may seem like a foolish thing to say, but most importantly, know what your book is about and be able to explain it within two or three sentences. I'm sure that when people have asked you, "What's your book about?" you tend to stumble over a vague explanation, backtrack, and then finally say, "But there's really much more to it than that."

Admittedly, that was one of the more difficult aspects for me when it came to talking about *Without Grace*. I wanted my readers to know that it was about so much more than a family whose mother walked out on them, but by the time I was into the full-blown synopsis, I could see the eyes of my listeners suddenly glaze over. You will get the same reaction if you don't have a pitch prepared to present to venue managers and the media. Therefore, while you're writing your book and strategizing, consider the pitch.

The best story I can use to explain this one is how the movie *Alien* had been pitched to producers. According to the story, they didn't go into a long scenario. Instead, they simply said, "Think *Jaws* in outer space."

Pretty good, huh?

Therefore, as you are chiseling your synopsis into three strong sentences, you will begin to pull your hair out, but it will be worth it. (Besides, there have been great strides taken to combat hair loss!) Fortunately, the editors at iUniverse were able to help me whittle down my verbose synopsis to this:

> *Without Grace* is a heartening portrait of small-town life and a tender and triumphant coming-of-age tale about the complexities and comforts of family and the healing that comes with letting go of the past.

Yes, it's so much more, but that one sentence encapsulates the mood and storyline well enough to whet the appetite; so much so that I was able to get media, articles, and events from this one sentence.

FINDING YOUR AUDIENCE

I recently met Judy Bolton and Wendy Bolton Floyd when they attended an event that I was doing. They were both in identical black T-shirts emblazoned with this bright pink question: *When did you know he was not the one?* After my event, I had the opportunity to chat with them and discovered that these two sisters would be publishing a book in February of 2007 with the title that they were promoting on their shirts. I asked if I could interview them for this book.

Wendy, a writer and graduate of Queens College, and her sister Judy, a Columbia University graduate with a background in clinical psychotherapy, came up with the idea for their book twelve years ago. Talk about perseverance! Once they committed themselves to the idea, they knew they needed a platform. They also knew they had to find their market *before* writing the book. For quite some time now, they have made it their business to wear their T-shirts out in public, and, invariably, people ask about them. Wendy said that the book is a grassroots effort, one in which they interviewed women from all walks of life, asking the title question of their book: *When Did You Know ... He Was Not the One?* (iUniverse). As for events, they plan to begin holding them around Valentine's Day, because "not everyone is going to have a date." For these events, they explained that they planned to have some "whine and cheese"—yes, that kind of *whine*—as well as the kind from the fermented grape.

Not only that, their Web site (www.whendidyouknow.net) is already up and has a number of important links. Now, mind you, prior to the book's publication, they were already invited to do a workshop for Parents Without Partners. Judy said that the workshop would be easy since they know the topic very well. She also advised authors to "always be ready" to talk about their book and to have a copy handy, no matter where they go.

The determination of these two women confirmed the message I got from my fortune cookie just the other day: a window of opportunity won't open itself. (I use my favorite fortunes as a bookmark, and that one was no exception!)

If Judy and Wendy hadn't seen the need to begin promoting their book before it was published, they would not be mentioned here. Word of mouth is one of your best promoters, but you have to give people something to talk about.

Gerard F. Bianco had an audience in mind, too, when he wrote his mystery *The Deal Master* (iUniverse). When I interviewed Bianco, he told me that he had done his homework, but it became obvious to me as we were talking that inspiration was also his motivator. Here is a brief bio that can be found from Bianco's Web site, www.gerardfbianco.com:

> Gerard F Bianco was born and raised in Brooklyn, New York. Smoky pool halls, Irish bars, and Italian social clubs are some of the local hangouts that have influenced his writing.

Bianco took the influences of these very real pool halls and bars and gave them a place in his novels, which was a shrewd marketing tool. When it came time to book events, instead of trying to succeed in a bookstore setting, Bianco contacted managers of the actual restaurants in his novel. He had made it clear to the managers that the events would in fact be promoting the restaurants and not just *The Deal Master*. In March of 2006, Bianco held an event at a restaurant in Portland, Maine. Bianco said that the restaurant sent out invitations to their mail list. Soon after, Bianco had another event in New York City. I have included the invitation that was sent out from the Duane Park Café, one in which I RSVP'd positively.

When I arrived at the restaurant, Bianco was at the front door greeting his guests. He then introduced me to Marisa Ferraria, general manager for Duane Park Café. Ferraria said that the restaurant had invited those on their mail lists, and they had handed out postcards promoting the event at the front desk where the host received customers. There was also an announcement in the weekly, well-read magazine *Time Out New York*. Guests reserved a seat for the event for $55, which included wine, a three-course mystery dinner, and gratuity. The restaurant holds sixty patrons, and fifty-eight guests RSVP'd favorably.

The evening could not have been lovelier and was filled with laughter, which was important to the author. Bianco said he had been to book events where he witnessed people drifting off due to how uneventful it was. He wanted to be sure his guests would be entertained. Besides having to guess what Chef Seiji Maeda had prepared for the mystery dinner—and, no, it wasn't anything bizarre, but a

"The Duane Park Café is a charming little restaurant . . ."

GERARD F BIANCO

THE DEAL MASTER

A Novel

...exactly what Gillette needed to help him forget the investigation."
Excerpt from the award-winning novel
The Deal Master

Duane Park Café presents:

Murder, Mystery & Meal

Monday, June 26th, 6 p.m.

Chef Seiji Maeda will create a 3 course mystery dinner ($55 including wine, gratuity and tax) paired with wine. Diners will guess what they are eating and drinking to win a dinner for 2 and a free copy of *The Deal Master* which features Duane Park Café.

Author, Gerard Bianco will be here to share secrets on How to Commit (to writing) The Perfect Murder (mystery).

Duane Park Café · 157 Duane St. NYC
Reservations required: 212-732-5555
www.duaneparkcafe.com

The Deal Master is available at BarnesandNoble.com, Amazon.com, or www.thedealmasternovel.com

rather delicious fare—diners were given an amusing slide presentation on what it was like to be a mystery writer. Bianco did not read from his book because he felt those who purchased it could do that on their own. And purchased they did. There were stacks of books available, and the author managed to circle the room to autograph copies for the jovial crowd.

Bianco was right when he said that he didn't just do signings, which meant he gave his audience something more. Apparently, this author knew his audience for this book. He not only planned what he was going to do but executed it. So, remember, it's all about figuring out the time, place, and subject that will draw your target audience to you. The event itself will be your opportunity to hook your audience and persuade them to buy your book.

Gordie Little has been a well-known radio personality in the North Country for thirty-five years. He now writes a weekly column for *The Press Republican*, but he also writes children's stories in hopes of seeing them published one day. His first book is titled *A Gittle's a Gittle,* and he has two more in the series. Even though he hasn't sought a publisher just yet for them, he is marketing them by doing readings at local schools in the area. This provides Gordie the opportunity to test his market, and he's discovered that the response has always been enthusiastic.

For the adult market, Gordie collects real ghost stories and shares them with audiences of various ages. Gordie knows that building a fan base is half the battle, and, when it comes time to sell his published works, he will have done just that. Name recognition is one way to reach readers, and that is just what this man is doing.

But what if you aren't writing a children's book or have your own built-in fan base? What then? How do you test the market?

Building Your Platform

Lynn Andriani interviewed literary agent Madeleine Morel for the May 29, 2006, issue of *Publishers Weekly*.[1] Morel represents only ghost-writers. In the interview, this savvy agent said that by the early 2000s, it had become evident that the "platform had become the sine qua non of selling nonfiction." Morel had an epiphany when she came to understand that plenty of people with inadequate writing skills were getting book deals because they had a platform.

However, this is not just one person's opinion.

The June 5, 2006, issue of the *New York Observer* had an article by Sheelah Kolhatkar titled "If You Build It, They Will Come—Hot in Publishing: Platforms!"[2] In this article, literary agent Todd Shuster said that "Competing as number one publicity marketing criterion for publishers these days are platform and prior sales."

Platform and *prior sales* are dilemmas for most first-time novelists, and I was well aware of that while I was writing my novel *Without Grace*, since I had booked author events for a local bookstore and then became the national event specialist for the bookchain for a number of years.

When I first booked events, I began to see that it was simply a revolving door of authors coming and going. Each one would come in, and, if he or she wasn't just sitting behind a table doing a signing, the author would stand in front of a smattering of people sitting in chairs, do a reading from their book, take a couple of questions, and then sign any copies that hopefully were purchased. I took mental notes, seeing what worked and what didn't. When I began writing my novel, I strategized how I was going to get it in as many hands as possible. My Rolodex was expanding and the business cards piling up, but I was also considering what my platform should be. Sure, *Without Grace* is a work of fiction, and finding a platform for fiction can be difficult. In addition, since I did

---

1   Lynn Andriani, "Ghost Stories," *Publishers Weekly*, May 5, 2006
2   Sheelah Kolhatkar, "If You Build It, They Will Come—Hot in Publishing: Platforms!," *New York Observer*, June 5, 2006

not have a recognizable name, I needed to build my platform from the ground up. However, I was not going to allow those two minor details stop me. So what did I do?

The novel takes place in a very small town in upstate New York called Churubusco (pronounced chairabusko). That curiously named town is where I actually grew up. I knew that it would be relatively easy to promote the novel in my hometown, even though I hadn't lived there for well over thirty years, because I still have family there. However, I needed to figure out my gameplan beyond those borders. So while writing, actually, rewriting the novel, I realized that I could reach out to missing-person organizations, since the novel deals with a missing mother. Also, one of the characters in *Without Grace* is an environmentalist who is eager to protect his small town from being commercialized by a shrewd entrepreneur. I kept that issue in the back of my mind, as well. In addition to those possible audiences, my protagonist has a strong interest in becoming another Julia Child. Cooks and chefs could be another possible market. Later, in the events section, I will share some of the events I did and how I booked them.

My point is, while you are writing your book, consider the possibile markets, all the while considering if an event would make sense or not. Julie Bosman, in the November 2, 2006, issue of the *New York Times* had an article titled "Peddling Books, From the Carwash to the Boutique." In part, she writes:

> Publishers hope to revive sagging book sales by pushing their titles in unusual outlets, such as car washes, butcher shops, clothing boutiques and hardware stores; odd venues have become fastest growing component in many major publishers' retail strategies in recent months; new frontier is being explored after years of concentrating on big-box retailers and online retailers; total number of books sold outside bookstores is imposible to discern, but publishing houses know it has affected their bottom

line; Simon & Schuster's special market sales, as they are called, have grown by 50 percent, surpassing total sales to independent bookstores.

This same marketing strategy can be used when trying to do events for your book. For instance, if you are writing a book about cars, trucks, tractors, or anything that runs with an engine, I would begin strategizing to see how you could do an event at your local AutoZone, Pep Boys Auto, or any other automotive store. If your book is about a boy and his dog, instead of trying to do an event at your local bookstore, consider your local pet store. And while you are at it, research your local animal shelter and take a break from writing your book to write a letter to the American Society for the Prevention of Cruelty to Animals, letting them know that you plan to donate a percentage of sales from your book to their cause. Don't freak out, since the possible media attention received from this will be worth it in the long run, but I'll discuss this in more detail later on.

It doesn't matter if your book is fiction or non, if you acquaint yourself with the traffic patterns of the venues for an event you believe would work, you will be acquiring information that will help you strategize; information is empowering.

Chapter 2

GATHERING INFORMATION

While you are working on your book, keep your eyes and ears opened for possible locations for an event. Then, once you are in the final editing phase of your book, begin to implement your mental plan of attack. Whether you are going to schedule a cross-country tour or keep it local, you will need to plan accordingly.

Planning means educating yourself about the foot traffic at the venues you think may be a great location for your events. The more information you have about the venue the better. Questions to ask yourself are

- Who is their audience or patron?

- What events did or didn't work in the past?

- Why would they take time to book you?

By answering these questions, when you approach the manager, he or she will be impressed that you've made an effort to understand their demographics, which may be convincing enough to let you schedule an event there. If you approach the manager without a clue about the clientele, you will be doing both the venue and yourself a disservice, and wasting everyone's time.

EXPLORE THE POSSIBILITIES

Even the most seasoned authors need to go where their audience is instead of relying on the masses coming to them. Granted, if this will be your first published book it will be more difficult, so take advantage of the experiences of others that I'll be sharing.

Most authors are under the impression that the bookstore setting is the zenith for events. Bear in mind, though, that since I had been booking events for so long, over the years I began to witness an interesting, if not confounding, dynamic: bookstores quite often are not the best location to do a book event. This can quite often be the case for authors at every stage of their career, even those with a firm platform.

The bookstore I worked in had three levels. One could easily have gotten lost in it; in fact, some customers did. However, when trying to figure out what events would work for the store, I would check the sales of the many different genres. If there was one genre that didn't move very well, it was a good indication that an event would not necessarily work. However, a particular genre that sold well was no guarantee for a successful event either. Again, it's a paradox, but in order to give yourself the best chance of success for your book, I suggest going to your market instead of trying to entice your market to come to you.

The media has been writing about this for the last few years while publishers are trying to figure out the reason for this phenomenon.

FOR YOUR CONSIDERATION

In the June 5, 2006, issue of *Publishers Weekly*,[3] Rachel Deahl wrote about author Greg Palast's book tour:

> Author Greg Palast managed to put his first book, *The Best Democracy Money Can Buy*, on the bestsellers lists thanks in part

---

3   Rachel Deahl, "Palast Thinks Outside the Bookstore, On Tour," *Publishers Weekly*, June 6, 2006

to an imaginative tour that took him away from the traditional venue stops: bookstores. At packed speaking engagements in churches, movie theaters and other venues, Palast was able to draw audiences sympathetic to his left-leaning message.

Palast is a recognizable name, and he was smart enough to know that he needed to bring his message to the people, instead of hoping that the people would come to him. Not only was his tour imaginative, but it was nontraditional. Think about the following question as you are reading through this book: What venues other than a bookstore would make sense for your book; if not a church, then what about a casino?

In the June 23, 2006, issue of the *New York Times*, Motoko Rich wrote an article titled "Casinos to Book Lovers: Let Us Entertain You, Too."[4] In the article, Rich writes:

> Publishers are constantly looking for ways to increase exposure for their writers and increase sales. Bookstore readings, while still a mainstay, are now being supplemented by appearances at fashion stores, corporate headquarters, and even at car dealerships. Casinos are just the latest, glitziest addition to that list.

However, earlier, the May 16, 2006, issue of the *New York Times* had another article by Rich titled "Authors Meet Fans Far From Bookstores, at Company Events."[5] Publicity director for Scribner, an imprint of Simon & Schuster, Suzanne Balaban was quoted in this article as saying, "It is easier to get people through the eye of a needle into the kingdom of heaven than it is to get people into a bookstore at 7 o'clock at night."

---

4   Motoko Rich, "Casinos to Book Lovers: Let Us Entertain You, Too," *New York Times*, June 23, 2006

5   Motoko Rich, "Authors Meet Fans Far From Bookstores, at Company Events," *New York Times*, May 5, 2006

A Paradox

It's a curious matter, because, even though bookstores carry books, they aren't always the best place to hold author events. This is something for you to consider while strategizing. Therefore, according to the *New York Times* article, authors are combating the trend by doing readings and signings at companies where their friends and families work. Kim Ricketts has been coordinating author readings at companies and nonprofit groups for several years. It has expanded from organizing five readings a month to anywhere from twenty to thirty. I was so impressed with what Ricketts had been doing for authors that I contacted her to discuss her *modus operandi* in more detail.

Ricketts has been in the business of books for quite some time. She had been both a book club coordinator and an events and programs coordinator for an independent bookstore in Seattle, Washington. During the five years that she held the latter post, she discovered that large offsite lecture venues were guaranteed to have successful author events. Therefore, in 2003 Ricketts founded Kim Ricketts Book Events, a company dedicated to connecting authors and books with readers in a wide variety of nontraditional venues—from corporate campuses to cocktail parties. Ricketts works with many major publishers, so I asked if she ever booked authors who were self-published.

"Yes," she said. "I keep a file of authors and the topics they cover so that if a venue has a specific need, I may be able to schedule that particular author."

Ricketts has found a market for authors and their books, and it was Malcolm Gladwell, author of *The Tipping Point*, who said that the way Ricketts managed to get the books in the hands of influentials was the very idea of *The Tipping Point*. I absolutely concur, but Ricketts' Web site (www.kimricketts.com) says it best:

> We are an entirely new type of bookseller, creating events in
> a variety of non-traditional venues and seeking out exciting

new places for readers and authors to connect. With years of bookselling and event planning experience, we are able to bring fascinating authors to your workplace, party, school or workshop, and coordinate all aspects of the event. In the past two years we have coordinated a wide variety of events, including: public chef dinners and noontime "chef chats", large political events, workshops, ongoing corporate author series, multi-day conferences, cocktail parties, fundraisers and more. If you are interested in adding books and authors to your workplace and your life, call us!

Go Where the Money Is

In this same vein, I also interviewed CEO of Powerhousepr Inc., Farris Rookstool III, who had worked as a district marketing manager for one major bookstore chain and a manager for another before creating his own PR firm. Rookstool said that "book signings in traditional bookstores are an old school approach to selling books."

He continued with that theme by saying that whether it is the author or a PR person that they have hired, the event needs to be properly promoted. With his experience working in the traditional bookstore setting, he has wondered why an author would do an event where there is little support.

"Our experience," Rookstool III said, "is to use the bank robber Willie Sutton rule when at all possible. 'Go where the money is.' If you can have your event where everyone attended to see you, then you will sell more books."

Powerhousepr Inc. was hired in October 2005 by the *Dallas Morning News* newspaper to produce their book *Eyes of the Storm: Hurricanes Katrina and Rita: A Photographic Story* with a special introduction by Cokie Roberts. Since the net proceeds for this book were to benefit charity, producing the book expeditiously was of the utmost importance. Rookstool III proved that even with little turnaround time, by producing the book in less than twelve days, with a marketing plan in place, the book was a success.

"How do you convince people to purchase a book that does not provide them entertainment or pleasure?" asks Rookstool, during our conversation. "Who wants to come to a book signing focusing on such a tragedy? After giving this much thought, we came up with a vehicle where companies could purchase sponsorships for the book while having their company name listed on *The Dallas Morning News* Web site, in turn donating their purchased copies to nonprofit organizations, schools and churches."

Besides getting a glowing review from former president George H. W. Bush, images from *Eyes of the Storm* won the 2006 Pulitzer Prize for Breaking News Photography.

One final thought that Rookstool III imparted was that if authors want to sell a large quantity of books, they must determine who their audience is.

Both Ricketts and Rookstool know that having a built-in audience with guaranteed sales, and very little second-guessing equals a successful event. And everyone wants a successful event.

Chapter 3

_____

MAKING CONTACTS

ABOUNDING RESOURCES

Most authors are members of writer organizations, and, if you are not, I strongly encourage you to put this book down briefly and research the organizations in your community. I am fortunate to live in an area where I could join a long line of organizations, but, presently, due to lack of time, I am an active member in only two: the International Women's Writing Guild (IWWG) and Women's National Book Association (WNBA). Both organizations have chapters throughout the country, and I strongly encourage you to see if they are near where you live, since they offer support and encouragement for writers at any stage in their career. However, there are a number of other possible organizations, too many to provide a list here, but a search on the Internet will give you an idea of what is out there. From romance to speculative to nonfiction, there is an organization that will offer the help you need. They will also be a great way to promote events, from listing your events on their Web site to having other members attend in support of a fellow writer. (Yes, we are a rather supportive group, to be sure!)

Besides accessing writing organizations, there are an unlimited number of resources that are easy to tap into, thanks to the Internet. One such association I encourage you to peruse online is the National Council of

Women's Organizations www.womensorganizations.org. According to their Web site, NCWO is a nonpartisan, nonprofit umbrella organization of groups that collectively represent over ten million women across the United States. Their members collaborate through substantive policy work and grassroots activism to address issues of concern to women, including workplace and economic equity, education and job training, affirmative action, Social Security, childcare, reproductive freedom, health, and global progress for women's equality.

It would be to your advantage to find out what members are located in your region and to try to get on their calendar to schedule a talk based on your book. There must be some angle that your book could work to address one or more of these organizations.

Do Your Homework

I interviewed S. H. Post, author of *samsara moon* (Kirk House Publishers), since he has managed not only to get restaurants to host his events but to involve a charity. Post's book is historical fiction, and I wondered why restaurants and a charity wanted to get involved.

Having a *local* restaurant host a book event isn't as difficult as booking one out of the neighborhood, but, besides getting Post's local Long Island restaurant to host an event, the author was also able to book one in Fairfield, Connecticut, one in Chicago, Illinois, and another in Boston, Massachusetts. How did he do it? Post did his homework. He initially targeted venues with either a history of literary events or those for which he had referrals and personal connections, and there is nothing wrong with using personal connections. The restaurants chose not to charge to have the events because they wanted to participate in the charitable cause. The Center for HOPE is a Long Island organization that provides grief counseling and bereavement support to area children who've lost a parent. It wasn't by chance that Post selected this cause. Not only does his novel deal with this topic, but it is also something his children know all too well.

I asked Post, "When did you begin to reach out to this organization?"

He responded, "My first meeting with the Center for HOPE was even before I had a final deal with my publisher. It was still in evaluation. I represented that what I was proposing was a possibility, but not definite. I began planning the book launch events soon after understanding the publisher's calendar and time frame for release and pub dates."

Did you catch that? Post was preparing for his book events even *before* he had a firm book deal.

He continued. "In the meeting, I shared my vision, my background, and the commonality to their cause. I believe a charitable focus has to seem relevant to the attendees and general public, and make sense to those running the charity. Otherwise, there is a risk that it is nothing more than a marketing plan. When my first wife died, the organization's support to my children and myself was a lifeline, and the people at the Center for HOPE heard my sincerity. With their agreement I received full use of their logos and was allowed to link to their Web site."

It was vision that helped Post strategize while he was writing his book.

By the way, how did I come to know S. H. Post? *He* contacted *me*. He read about me and saw that I was on the advisory council for the New York Center for Independent Publishing, as well as the Writer's Conference Committee. Post found my Web site and contact information and introduced himself via e-mail. After I responded, he invited me out to a nice restaurant for lunch to discuss his book and the marketing plan for it, looking for any advice I could give him, which wasn't much since he had a strong sense of how to market his novel. I could tell that he was passionate about his writing, and I believe that passion was how he managed to get others involved.

To reiterate the strategy that Post had implemented, I recently spoke to Debbi Honorof, associate executive director for marketing and development for Friends of the Arts on Long Island. She also writes for *Long Island Woman* magazine. Honorof had been the events coordinator for an independent bookstore several years ago and has been working in the field of nonprofit marketing, PR, and special events for many years. I asked her if she thought that book events were as successful as they once were. Her response was that with all the competition of on-demand movies and the number of programs available, book events had to find a way to get publicized. Honorof felt that it would only benefit an author to "hook up with a nonprofit organization."

Gene Taft, former vice president, assistant publisher, and director of publicity at PublicAffairs Publishers, agreed. Taft recently moved to Washington DC to start his own PR firm (http://www.genetaftpr.com/). When I asked him what had been some of the best events he had scheduled over the years, he said the ones where there had been a partnership. He then mentioned that one author had worked with the World Affairs Council, and, due to a specialized audience, the event had been a success. However, Taft said, "Without a doubt, authors have to hustle to get an audience." He then went on to add that if authors believe the publisher is supposed to sell their books, there will be problems. Today's author needs to be a marketing guru.

If you can manage to find an organization to work with that will be beneficial to both their cause and your book, try to make it happen. It will be a win-win situation and a springboard to success.

SEEKING BLURBS

There was something else I didn't mention during my lunch meeting with author S. H. Post. He'd brought his press kit and an advanced reader's copy of his book to the lunch meeting. I couldn't help but notice that, even though Little Brown was not the publisher of Post's novel, Michael Pietsch, the senior VP of Little Brown, had given *samsara moon* a nice blurb. (If you've never heard this term before, a *blurb* is simply the words of praise that can be found on book jackets.) I asked Post how that had transpired, and he said that even though Pietsch had liked the book, in the end he had decided not to publish it; however, he had written some kind words about it. Post had implemented it in his package, proving that rejection doesn't always have to be negative. He then asked me if I would read *samsara moon* and perhaps give him my own blurb for the book. He was laying the groundwork for success. Something that I, too, had done when preparing to publish my novel.

Because I had had the opportunity to work with many authors over the years, I managed to make friends with quite a number of them. And while I am a strong believer in using one's resources, I never wanted to cross the line of unprofessionalism while being on my company's clock, so I had kept my personal aspirations of publishing a novel to myself until it had come up in a conversation with my author friends. Eventually, though, when the novel had been in its final editing stages, I had begun querying some of these friends to see if they would take the time to read *Without Grace* and be willing to give me some words of praise. Even though *Without Grace* is mainstream fiction, I got nice blurbs from independent journalist Author Kent, philosopher and editor Elliot D. Cohen, PhD, self-help author Susan Shapiro Barash, and raconteur and memoirist Malachy McCourt. Fiction writers Michael Malone, Rona Jaffe, and Martha Randolph Carr rounded out the impressive group.

Like Post and myself, you too can get blurbs for your book. It's not as difficult as it may seem. These blurbs do not have to be from recognizable names—although that would help—but should be from people who are qualified to give an opinion. For instance, if your book is a psychological thriller, try to get a blurb from a psychologist that states that your characters are true to form, making the story believable. The validation of qualified people will add credibility to you as a writer and to your book while catching your coveted readers' attention.

But how do you go about asking for a blurb?

Since you will not have a finished copy of your book, you will need to send your manuscript to the appropriate contact. However, first query to be sure the contact has the time or interest to read your manuscript (be it in its entirety or a portion) to give the desired praise. See if any of your friends know someone who may be able to help you, so that you may first introduce yourself through that association. That was how I managed to get a blurb from author Michael Malone. His cousin, Peggy Zieran, is a close friend of mine, so she shot him an e-mail and asked if he'd be interested. She also told him that he wouldn't be wasting his time, since the book is worthy of praise. (Hey, I'm not making that up!)

But back to you. Consider querying someone who attended the same alma mater as you, since that will give you a likely advantage. Also, find out as much about the prospective contact as you can, and, when you are querying the possible "blurber," let him or her know why you would be honored to have words of praise from them in your book. Trust me, it will be well worth your time.

Hire a Web Designer

We are in a new era, and the Internet is an all-important tool that you must use to find your audience. Don't wait until your book is published to begin the process, since it may take longer than you expect: from finding a designer, getting a domain name, and creating the site. If you have the tech know-how, you may be able to manage all the details, but, if you are like me, you will need to shop for a Web designer and make sure he or she is right for you. Check out some of the sites a prospective Web designer has established and see what you like or dislike about them. A designer will be able to set you up with your unique domain name. Just what is a domain name? A domain name is simply your site's Web address. For instance, mine is www.carolhoenig.com. Go ahead, put the book down, and take a look at it. I can wait.

Now that you are back, let me tell you that I worked with the designer to purposely color coordinate the site with the cover of my novel. Also, since my byline is in a variety of different publications, I figured using my name for the address made more sense than using the title of my book, especially since I knew I'd be publishing more than one book. However, the key is to find a Web address that makes sense for you.

As for the content on the site, once you have your book cover, make sure that the image is on the first page of the site. In the beginning, you won't have too much information for your site; however, you could include a teaser from your book as well as any words of praise—even if it's from friends. But as you are ready to promote your book, the most important information to post on your site is your events, and keep it updated. Depending on your time and the designer's time, you could also keep an online journal or blog and provide updates to your fan base about your book, your book tour, and any other publications you have. But other than friends and family, who will know about your site?

THE ENGINE THAT COULD

Having your mom or cousin talk up your Web site is a start, but it cannot end there. That would be like driving a car along a single-lane road with little traffic. What you want is to open up a four-lane expressway, with your Web site being the destination. There are a number of ways to do this.

Imagine your book is about jazz, and someone uses the keyword *jazz* in their Google or Yahoo search, but it takes several pages before your Web site comes up—if at all. That's like having a detour on that highway. In a conversation with a friend recently, she said that she rarely goes beyond page three in her keyword searches. I tend to dig a little deeper, but most people are satisfied with what they find by page ten. Your job is to make sure that keywords based on your book come up in those first ten pages. You will need to discuss with your Web designer how to take advantage of the search engine keywords, and be specific. If your book is about a particular jazz artist, then use that artist's name as a keyword; however, expect to pay for the service. Over time, chances are those keywords will be working for you and driving more traffic to your site and in turn helping with sales of your book.

Gotta Card?

A couple of years ago, a literary magazine published an essay I wrote titled "Gotta Card?" It was about how people often ask that very question upon meeting in a business setting, then they tuck the card in their pocket for safe keeping until they get home or back to their office and then file it away for possible future reference. So let me ask you, "Gotta card?"

At this point I hope I have made my point that marketing your book is pretty much going to be your responsibility, so it only makes sense for you to have a business card. It doesn't have to be fancy or flowery, but it does have to be concise. Besides your name and the title of your book, you should include your Web site and e-mail address on your business card. In all honesty, I didn't include my e-mail address. I put the Web site address on it, and, every time I handed over my card, I let people know that there was a link to contact me. By doing so, I drove traffic to my site before it got redirected to my e-mail.

Also, you may want to put a few words of praise on your card, if there is room and doesn't look too busy. Some people invest in cards that have the image of their book, but, if money is an object, keeping it simple works just as well. I know of other authors who prefer to use bookmarks with the image from their book as a business card. I don't have a preference, but you may.

Who would have thought that writing a book was so complicated? It doesn't have to be as long as you approach it as a business, one that belongs to you. This book is to help you in that process. Now it's almost time to take that giant step, but first let's recap what needs to occur *before* you publish. But, as a caveat, this does not mean that once your book is out the work is almost over. Actually, what you've done up to this point is pave a path using a detailed map, but it's a path that you will need to travel consistently. But fortunately the road will be familiar, and there will be less chance of getting lost. Also, many of the items to do before you publish can be done simultaneously.

RECAP

- Create an events strategy

- Consider who your market or audience is

- Maintain your list of contacts

- Update your Rolodex

- Define your book in two or three sentences

- Find and build your platform

- Join and network with organizations in your area

- Consider possible venues for your events

- Decide whether it would make sense to work with a charity in support of your book

- Get words of praise or blurbs

- Hire a Web designer

- Think about search engine keywords based on your book

- Have business cards printed

By now, I hope it is evident that it takes time, energy, and work to organize events for your book. However, after you have done a couple of events, you will find that they will get easier and less stressful, and you will become more flexible. The next part of the book will give you specific timelines and guidelines in planning your events. Each writer will need to tweak the plans to fit for his or her book, so bear in mind that the timeline and guidelines are simply to show you how to proceed. It's up to you to do so.

Ready? Let's begin.

Part 2

YOU HAVE A DUE DATE!

Chapter 4

DEFINING EVENTS

Writing a book can be a laborious, lonely, and lengthy process, but it is also one that expresses your creativity. Therefore, upon publication, you should announce it to the world and celebrate what you've accomplished! Celebrate means more than a simple book signing.

Note that book signings, book events, and book launches are three different types of occasions; how you approach each will dramatically affect the turnout.

Book *signings* consist of the author sitting at a table and autographing his or her book for those who have purchased a copy. It's usually a quiet and uneventful affair.

Book *events* include a discussion by the author where chairs are set up for a hopeful audience, followed by a signing. Those who attend this type of occasion get to know the author better and have an opportunity to converse in more detail about the book. This is an opportunity for the author to endorse his or her book so that everyone in attendance will want to buy a copy—and maybe even an extra as a gift.

Book *launches* are more celebratory and occur soon after the publication of your book. They can be executed in a variety of ways. Later, I will provide several examples of actual successful book launches. The exciting news is that you have a publication date for your book and you've been busy creating a strategy. Now it's time to act on it. First, though, you must ask yourself: is an event right for my book?

EVENTS: SHOULD YOU DO THEM?

If you know who you are marketing your book to, you will know if it makes sense to do an event for it or not. One clear example that I can offer is from my own experience as an events coordinator for a major bookstore chain in Manhattan. Daily, several authors eager to do events in my store would approach me, but there was one author in particular whom I won't forget. I do not recall the title of the book, but I will never forget the subject matter, which was the joy of menstruation intended for preadolescent girls. The author sent me a copy of the book, with illustrations of a flower blooming and a detailed explanation about what happens when a young girl becomes a woman. The author wasn't a doctor or expert in the subject, and the book confirmed it. Besides, I worked in a midtown Manhattan store where we rarely got a young audience for any event, and I couldn't imagine preadolescent girls being willing to come to a store to have a woman talk to them about such an intimate topic in front of customers browsing the shelves nearby.

And, admittedly, I could not imagine having to announce the event over the paging system of the store, since the title left no question as to what the book was about.

I turned down the event proposal.

Even if the author's book had been more professional, it was unlikely that I would have booked her for an event. Nevertheless, most authors would know that doing an in-store event on such a personal topic is most likely a waste of everyone's time. That is not to say that the book is a waste, but doing events for it would be, since it is doubtful anyone would show up.

ADVICE TO HEED

To confirm what I have just said, Judith Rosen wrote an article in the October 9, 2006, issue of *Publishers Weekly* titled "Turning Book Signings Into Profit Centers."[6] In the article, she quotes Paul Bogaards, executive director of publicity for Knopf Publishing Group at Random House, who was asked about touring authors. He said, "Like parents, the most important decision publishers and booksellers are reaching these days is often the decision to say, 'No.'"

Therefore, consider the book you've written. If you can envision an engaged audience who would be willing to sit through your presentation and participate in discussion, then chances are an event would be something to consider. If you've written a slim book with daily quotes or a book similar to the one mentioned above about a more private topic, I'd put my energy in promotion and marketing and forget doing events. For the rest of you who believe you have a platform and that events would be advantageous, let's begin considering the possibilities.

---

6   Judith Rosen, "Turning Book Signings Into Profit Centers," *Publishers Weekly*, October 9, 2006

Chapter 5

APPROACHING VENUES

Whether your book has a scheduled publication date or is already available, you need to strategize in advance. First, let me give you two different scenarios so that you may see what works and what doesn't in securing an event.

Let's say there are two authors: one, by the name of Heather, has written a historical novel, and it is her first publication; another author, by the name of Roy, has also written a historical novel, and it is his first. Both Heather and Roy want to promote events for their novel, as well they should. Heather walks into her local bookstore one morning and asks to see the manager. After several minutes pass, Heather's tone is somewhat annoyed as she reminds the salesclerk that she's been waiting to see the manager for quite some time. Heather also reminds the clerk that she is a published author. Finally, a woman appears and introduces herself as the store manager, apologizing for making Heather wait but explaining that she had payroll issues that needed to be addressed right away.

Heather shakes the manager's hand and immediately lets her know about her published novel. She tells the manager that she wants to do an event in her store in three weeks. The manager suggests Heather leave her press kit, so that when she isn't quite so busy she could consider the possibility, but says that she doesn't book events with only a three-week lead time; two months is more like it. Heather questions why there would need to be a two-month lead time, since people will *definitely* come to the event.

The manager, who is being paged, tells Heather again to leave a press kit so that she can look at it when things aren't so crazy. She also mentions that making an appointment would have given her the ability to give Heather the attention she needed. Heather then says she doesn't have a press kit but suggests the manager check out her Web site. Heather scribbles the URL for her Web site on a scrap piece of paper that the manager has given her. She tells the manager that she hopes to hear from her soon, because another store in the area *definitely* wants to do an event with her. She hopes the entrepreneurial competition will encourage the manager to book an event. Heather then leaves feeling frustrated that the manager would be so dumb-witted not to want to schedule an event right away. After all, doesn't she want to make sales from Heather's novel?

Later that afternoon, Heather follows up with the bookstore manager to see if she has had a chance to check the Web site. The manager says that since she has had two booksellers call in sick and a customer service issue she needed to handle, she hasn't had a chance to check the Web site. Heather says she will call the next morning to follow up.

Earlier that week, the same manager had had an opportunity to go through her mail and had opened up a press kit from a first-time author by the name of Roy, who has written a historical novel. The cover letter had included all of Roy's contact information and a synopsis of the novel, but, more importantly, the letter had included information as to what Roy would do to bring people into the store. He had included a copy of the invitation that he would send out and mentioned the quantity. He had also listed media contacts that he planned to invite to the event. In addition, he had been in contact with the historical society in the area, since his book had relevant historical information. Roy had given an estimate of the number of people he hoped he could rally for his event. He had then said that he would follow up with a phone call in about a week to give the manager enough time to look over his materials. And he did.

The manager booked Roy for an event two months later, and, when Heather called the following morning, the manager told her that she had already booked a similar event and didn't have room for another. Heather then told the manager that she would never shop in her store and would make sure her friends didn't, as well. She then hung up by slamming down the phone.

Sounds rather foolish on Heather's behalf, doesn't it? Well, I dealt with these types of authors quite often when I was booking events, and I was amazed that they didn't see the harm they were doing to their fledgling career. However, instead of focusing on what Heather did wrong, let's consider what Roy did right.

- Roy showed that he valued the manager's time by sending a cover letter and press kit as an introduction.

- Roy provided information about what he would do for the venue:

  1. Prepared invitations.

  2. Had a media list where he would send an announcement.

  3. Contacted a major outside source that would support the event.

- Roy forewarned that he would call within a week's time to follow up.

- Roy followed up, as promised.

- Roy was courteous.

- Roy secured an event.

Therefore, no matter where you want to book yourself, respect the venue's schedule and be sure to let them know what you will be doing for them (and not the other way around). Remember: the less work the venue has to do, the better chance you will have in getting an event there.

Sabotaging Success

Heather didn't help her career by her unprofessional attitude, but sometimes there can be outside circumstances that can hurt an event's success. Oftentimes, though, it's not necessarily *if* you build an event but *how* you build it that can affect the outcome. Let me share an actual situation about how a wife sabotaged her husband's event and quite possibly any future book deals for him—at least with one particular publisher.

This wife, who shall remain nameless, called me months before her husband's book was scheduled for publication and requested that I hold some dates on my calendar to book him for an event. She felt that the bookstore's location was impressive and would add cache to her husband's first book. I complimented her on providing me enough time for scheduling but told her that I would need to wait for an actual publication date, and then I would be happy to work with her husband's publicist. I had worked closely with this particular publisher and knew that they arranged tour schedules based on the media they could secure. I also knew that this particular publisher had other criteria for their authors and would not be pleased with interference from someone who didn't understand the business. Besides, I wasn't quite sure that we were the right venue for an event for this particular book and wanted to discuss that with the assigned publicist. About a week later, I received another call from the wife, wanting to know what I was doing to publicize her husband's event—an event that wasn't yet scheduled because the book still did not have a publication date.

Gently, I told the wife that I understood her enthusiasm and once again explained how the process worked. I also let her know that I was in discussions with the publicist, which I was, and that this publicist would contact me when she had more tour information.

A few weeks later, when the publicist knew what was being planned for the book by the marketing department (meaning what kind of budget was being set aside for this book), she called me, and it was decided that my store was not the ideal location for a number of reasons—one being that a competitor not too far away had already been scheduled to host the author as per the tour plans. The publicist called the wife and gave her the tour information, but the wife was adamant that her husband do an event in my store, as well. The wife called me behind the publicist's back to try and schedule something. Eventually, the publicist and I agreed to appease the wife in spite of our better judgment and suggested some possible dates, bearing in mind what would work for the store. Prior experience quickly revealed that most weekend and daytime events did not work. After a couple of e-mail exchanges, the publicist and I agreed on a weeknight that we believed would work for both the publisher and bookstore. (By this time, the publicist and I were swapping stories about the overzealous wife who thought she understood the publishing world.)

When I thought everything had been sorted out, I received another call from the wife, demanding that I book her husband for a lunchtime event instead of evening. She explained to me that, since the store was located in the business district of Manhattan, people would be certain to come to the event. I then countered that if it were a straight signing by a recognizably named author, there was a possibility it could work; however, that was not the case. I then explained that, since the book was geared for a discussion, doing the event in the evening when people wouldn't be in a rush to get back to the office would better serve the book and the store.

She would have none of it, and, after making persistent calls to both the publicist and myself, we allowed the wife to have her way. *Maybe* she knew something we didn't know. Even then, the phone calls did not stop. Almost daily, she would call asking what I was doing to promote the event. It was clear that my time meant very little to her. I explained what I was doing with both my budget and the co-op given from the publisher. (Co-op is money set aside by the publisher to promote specific titles. The money is used for advertising and prominent endcap, which is simply wall space at the end of a bookcase, and front-of-store displays.) I also reiterated my concern about hosting a lunchtime event, since those were rarely successful, but she dismissed me and said she was sure people would come.

I did the same promotion for her husband's event as I would do for every event I hosted in my store. I posted signs announcing the upcoming discussion, with a display of the books in several different locations of the store. I did a write-up in the newsletter. I sent out over fifty press releases. (Years ago, press releases were considered a great marketing tool, but, shortly, you will discover why that is no longer the case.) I also reminded the staff to mention it to the customers at the cash registers. I was unable to run an ad because there was not enough co-op to do so, which is quite often the case, especially for first-time authors. In this particular case, the co-op was fifty dollars, which I used to make posters and flyers. That said, every author I worked with was given a folder after his or her event or signing that included information of what I did to promote it. I would put copies of any ads run, the press release, and the list of where the release had been sent. On the day of the event, I made intermittent announcements over the intercom throughout the morning and had signs posted on the front doors. By lunchtime, chairs were set up along with the sound system in anticipation of a good turnout.

Unfortunately, no one showed up. Not one person.

It was the first interaction I'd had with the husband, and he was very kind and understanding. His wife, however, blamed me for the no-shows. She chastised me in front of her husband and any passing shoppers, demanding explanations for why no one showed up. I handed her the folder of what I had done to promote the event, while reminding her of the publicist's and my warnings. Her response was to huff off with her husband running after her. I never heard from her again.

Interestingly and amusingly, the book her husband had written was on the subject of how to avoid using curse words. Some things you just can't make up.

The above story shows what doesn't work and why. There is no guarantee that the event would have had a good turnout had I booked it in the evening, but it certainly would have been given a better shot. The book you are now holding will help you have that better shot.

More Info about Co-op

Did I hear you mumble something about the paltry fifty dollars given for co-op? You're right, that's not much money to promote an event, but, over time, I'd learned how to stretch that money to good use. One way was via a local radio program called *Books That Matter* that aired every Friday afternoon. Since it was a program about books, I was approached by the station for advertising dollars. Instead of giving money to promote just my store, I used the co-op and a bit more from my budget to promote my upcoming events for the following week. Eventually, I was invited to come on the program to talk about the upcoming events and began to cohost. I then included a tape of the show in the folder that I gave to the author, who would be thrilled that I had not only promoted the event but the book as well. That was one wise and beneficial way to use co-op.

Your Press Release

Chances are you have never written a press release before and have little idea what goes into one. Remember that the purpose of your press release is to not only announce your book's release but also to provide some key points that show why it is different from all the other books. This should make those you are sending it to want to know more about you and the book. Keep it simple enough that all the information is on one sheet, both front and back. The following should be included in the press release:

1. The name and address of your publisher at the top of the page. You may also want to use your publisher's logo.

2. On the upper left hand corner, put the words: FOR IMMEDIATE RELEASE along with the date.

3. If you are your own publicist, list your name and contact information, including your e-mail address, on the right hand side of the paper. Also, don't forget to include the title of your book and the ISBN (International Standard Book Number).

4. Next is your message, or your pitch. It should be no more than a paragraph or two. Remember, keep it simple but clear, engaging and enticing. Do *not* use phrases like, "No one has ever written anything so original!" or "Soon to be a bestseller!" Instead, keep it real while letting your book be your message. If you have a very strong sentence that illustrates why you were the best person to write the book, include that as well.

5. Hopefully, by now you have received some blurbs. Remember, these do not have to be from recognizable names, but should be from people who are qualified to give an opinion. This is also a good place to include any reviews you've received so far. It's true that early on you will have scarce material to include in your press release, but, if you do the work mentioned in previous chapters, you will soon be building your credits. This means that you will need to update your press release constantly. However, with a computer, it should be only a matter of tweaking. That said, be sure to read over each new press release to make sure you are not repeating yourself or omitting important information. Better yet, have a second set of eyes read it to catch those errors.

6. A one-paragraph bio is the next bit of information needed. If you have had experience speaking or doing interviews or with other publishing credits, be sure to include that. If you have not had experience, do not point it out for your reader. Instead, accentuate that you are up-and-coming. Imply that you are building momentum and excitement without going over the top. Again, be aware to whom

you are sending the press release and be certain that they are the right venue to approach. For instance, I heard about a local cable television show that aired in New York's tristate region. The interviewer, Dorothy Dunne, focused on travel on the program. Since I knew that Charlie Rose would not be interested in my fledgling novelist status, I decided to begin locally. This was my pitch to Ms. Dunne:

> An author tour can be fun, interesting, and even grueling. Why not interview an author who's booked herself all along the Eastern Seaboard and met some fascinating readers?

Remember, this interviewer focused mostly on travel. The moment she received my pitch, she contacted me and asked when I could be on the show. About a month later, when I was on, did we talk about my travel? Not much. We ended up talking about my novel. The exciting aspect was that I had just returned from BookExpo in Washington DC, where *Without Grace* had won Silver Medal for General Fiction for Book of the Year Award by *ForeWord* magazine, so Dorothy felt she had some bit of news by interviewing me.

MORE ABOUT PRESS RELEASES

Publicists use press releases all the time in an attempt to reach the media. Notice I said, "an attempt" to reach the media. Most of what is sent via e-mail is considered spam or electronic junk mail. Most of what is sent snail mail is tossed in the wastebasket without consideration. Therefore, do not be tempted to send your press release to every media outlet that has an e-mail, fax number, or post office address in hopes that at least a few will be interested to book you as a guest.

David Henderson, author of *Making News: A Straight Shooting Guide to Media Relations* (iUniverse Star),[7] says in his book that most press releases are a waste of everyone's time, since they do not offer news. Henderson says, "Veteran journalists generally have become wary of trivial fluff or blatantly commercial self-promotion under the 'news release' banner."

Henderson knows of what he speaks, since he is a writer, veteran public relations agency executive, and Emmy Award-winning former CBS news correspondent.

Unless your book addresses a current event that is in the news and you are adept at discussing it, avoid sending a press release to the media. However, releases *must* be a part of the press kit you send to possible event venues.

YOUR PRESS KIT

A press kit is an expanded press release, which is information collected into a sharp, clean folder. It must be professional so that you will be taken seriously. The number of press kits that I received when I was booking events taught me more what not to do than what to do. First, go to your local Staples or OfficeMax and buy a stack of folders with inside pockets and choose a color that complements your book cover. Have a professionally blown-up cover of your book sized to fit the folder. Attach it to the front of the folder without any bumps or tears. This will hold your press kit. Let's focus on what to include in it:

1. A well-written and concise press release.

2. A professional photograph of yourself.

3. Your bio, which can be more expansive than what you included in your press release.

---

7   David Henderson, *Making News: A Straight-Shooting Guide to Media Relations* (iUniverse Star 2006) 155.

4. Clear copies of reviews that are dated with the publication included, as well as any articles that have been written about you.

5. Blurbs or words of praise in their entirety, since you may have needed to cut them down for the press release. And don't forget to include the attribution to the blurb! Your readers need to know who appreciates what you've written.

6. A sheet of questions that would encourage anyone interested in hosting you to have an idea of what your book is about. Many publishers create what is known as a reading group guide, which provides questions for discussion. Even though it may not be as slick in appearance, you may do the same for your book and include it in the press kit.

7. A list of any speaking engagements you have done, and, if you have a copy of these engagements, whether audio or video, include that as well. This is where you could also offer information as to what you would be able to talk about at the event you are proposing to do.

The important thing is to remember that you are not the only author pitching to do events, and you must make your first impression a good one—rather a professional one. If your potential host feels that you are prepared and are offering something of value to the venue, he or she will more likely invite you to do an event.

Even though the following story is not about querying a venue for an event, it does show the difference between a good press kit and a bad one.

Since I am still promoting *Without Grace* while writing this book, I came across a call for submissions for books to review from *Girlistic Magazine*. However, before I dropped my novel in an envelope and sent it off, I researched their Web site (http://www.girlistic.com) to make sure that my novel would be right for them. After reading that the magazine focused on feminist thought and culture, I still wasn't quite sure, so I e-mailed the editor of the magazine and shared a bit about my novel, as well as myself. Editor Jaymi Heimbuch responded and felt that *Without Grace* would be something they would want to review and invited me to send her a copy.

Even though the book in your hands is about event planning, the same criterion applies whether an author is submitting a book for review or for a possible event. Here is a copy of the cover letter I'd sent:

July 24, 2006

Jaymi Heimbuch

Girlistic Magazine
721 E Main St #267
Santa Maria, CA 93454

Dear Ms. Heimbuch:

Thank you for inviting me to send *Without Grace* for review for *Girlistic Magazine*. I have enclosed a copy of my award-winning novel, as well as a press kit. Once you have looked over the materials, I look forward to hearing from you.

I wish both you and *Girlistic* much success!

Much appreciated,
Carol Hoenig

The letter wasn't too wordy, but it provided some key points:

1. The magazine *invited me* to send my novel.

2. It is an award-winning novel.

3. There is a press kit included.

4. I wished the magazine success.

A few days later, Jaymi e-mailed me the following:

Hello Carol,

I just wanted to let you know that I received your book today. I also wanted to compliment you on your professional package. I've received packages for review in all stages of disarray— including missing information, typos on the cover pages, or no cover pages at all. I already know part of the reason why your book has gone so far. I'm really looking forward to reading it in the next couple of weeks.

Talk to you soon,
Jaymi Heimbuch

I've been doing self-promotion for quite some time now, but that e-mail made my week! I knew that *Girlistic Magazine* was just starting out, but it has much potential when someone like Jaymi takes the time to send an e-mail as she did. And I didn't have to wonder if she'd received my materials. In turn, I asked Jaymi if I could interview her for this book, and she generously said yes.

First, I gave Jaymi an opportunity to share a bit about *Girlistic Magazine*. In one sentence, she encapsulated its mission: Our style is *Ms.* magazine meets *Bitch* magazine—edgy and intelligent. She then went on to answer my next question: What do you look for from authors who are sending you queries in support of their books? Jaymi's reply was insightful:

When artists send in requests for reviews, they usually send me information over e-mail or in snail mail. When I receive an e-mail, I can immediately tell which authors take themselves and *Girlistic Magazine* seriously, and which authors don't seem to care much about their first impression. I feel that the way an author presents themselves shows their level of respect to the magazine, and to themselves. So when I receive an e-mail, I expect them to introduce themselves, give me a run down of their book, let me know why they feel *Girlistic Magazine* is a fit for them, and then politely ask for a response. I expect it to be brief and easy to read.

One of my *biggest* peeves is when someone writes a one-sentence e-mail that says something like "I want you to review my book that comes out in two months. Let me know." And that's it. It makes me have to do a lot more work to find out if the book even fits in with our magazine. Most of the time I just ignore those letters because I simply don't have time to do the work for the author and weasel the necessary information out of them. When I receive a snail mail package, I expect at the very least a clean copy of their book with a cover letter that provides an introduction of themselves and their book, and why they want *Girlistic Magazine* to review it.

I've received packages with no cover letter, major misspellings (ex: "I am and new author ..."), and typos in the letter, a Post-it note tacked on to the cover of the book, bent or damaged books, and sometimes the book arrives weeks and weeks after they let me know they would be sending it.

Cover letters are *so* important because they remind me who the author is, and why I'm receiving their book. I get so many requests for reviews that it is sometimes difficult to keep track of the authors. The authors with great presentation get priority from me because they show an obvious respect for themselves and for my magazine.

What my ideal package looks like is an envelope that shows they care if I receive their book (delivery confirmation, priority mail, return receipt requested, or something of that nature), a clean, well-written cover letter, a clean copy of the book, copies of any other press the book has received, and other necessary information such as a bio of the author, list of other published works, etc.

Need I say more? Be sure to check out *Girlistic Magazine* and tell your friends about it.

Chapter 6

CHECK YOUR CALENDAR!

It takes a lot of energy and planning to schedule an event in support of your book, but there is no need to make it more difficult than necessary. When you are beginning to schedule events, be sure to have a calendar in front of you. Also consider referring to a school calendar from the markets where you want to do events. By doing this, your special event will not be in conflict with an important school event or PTA meeting. Besides Christmas being on December 25 and New Years on January 1, most other holidays have no particular set date, and you must be aware of that when booking yourself. This was a mistake I almost made.

I, along with the coordinator I was working with for one of my events, hadn't looked very closely at our calendars and initially scheduled an event at one particular store on Yom Kippur. Since the event was to be in a highly populated Jewish neighborhood, it would have been foolish, not to mention thoughtless, to attempt to make it happen. Fortunately, I caught it before I had sent out announcements, and we rescheduled. Besides no one showing up, I didn't want to be callous by booking something that would interfere with those celebrating the religious holiday.

Not only are national holidays something you need to be aware of, but you will also need to find out what other special events are going on in the markets where you plan to be. The Internet is extremely helpful in this research. Whether it is a firefighters' field day or a town's anniversary, you need to know what the competition will be. You will also need to know if these local events could work for or against you. For instance, if you are considering scheduling an event in a town during a street festival, you may want to reschedule.

On the other hand, you may want to book a table at the festival and hand-sell your book. You will need to have a discussion with someone from the town's chamber of commerce to get an idea of the demographics for the festival. Do people come for the carnival rides or to find deals from a variety of vendors? If the event is too late, too expensive, or doesn't make sense to rent space to sell your books, perhaps you could see if someone would walk around handing out flyers announcing your upcoming event that you scheduled during a less hectic and competitive time. (Of course, an incentive to encourage the person handing out the flyers would help. It doesn't have to be a large amount of money, but there should be some sort of compensation.)

The bookstore where I once scheduled events was only a couple of blocks from Manhattan's Fifth Avenue. Every fall on one September day, New York Is Book Country would close off Fifth Avenue for several blocks so that publishers and booksellers could set up booths and promote upcoming titles. Each year it felt like the entire world visited that long, legendary stretch, but, for some reason, there were authors who would want to schedule an event in the store on that particular day. Their thinking was that since there were thousands of people nearby, they could draw at least a percentage of them into the store. Unfortunately, they were wrong, and I would have to refuse them. What they did not understand was that, with the energy and excitement, New York Is Book Country was the place to be. However, if the author was a good fit for an event at the bookstore and I had enough advanced notice, I would include the event in the newsletter that was handed out to the huge crowd at the book fair. It was quite unlikely that many who looked at the newsletter would actually attend the event; however, it was a bit of promotion for the book and added cache to the author's résumé.

Jump on the Bandwagon

Just as there are times when you should avoid doing events, there are times of the year when you should be sure to jump on the bandwagon and participate. Most people know when the major holidays are and some people even know that Women's History Month is in March, but I bet you didn't know that January is Oatmeal Month or that September is Read-a-New-Book Month. Run to your library and pull out a copy of *Chase's Calendar of Events: The Day to Day Directory to Special Days, Weeks and Months.*[8] You will discover that there is National Craft Month and a Family History Month, as well as many other subjects that have been given a designated day.

So what does this have to do with you?

Well, there is bound to be a promotion that could fit in with the topic of your book. It doesn't matter if it's fiction or nonfiction. Take note though, that you will need to plan your promotion well in advance of these months in order to arrange events. If your book has a connection to crafts, contact your local craft store and see if you can set up an event with them. You may even get them to sponsor some advertising in support of the event. On the other hand, if you've written a book on your family history, contact your local historical society and see what kind of interest you will be able to generate. They may offer suggestions about when and where to have these events.

The point is, each month offers possibilities. If you cannot get your hands on *Chase's Calendar of Events* right away, I have listed some correlating designated dates at the end of this book.

Signings

As I previously stated, signings are simply a nonevent. They are set up so that you sit at a table and hope people stop by. Most often book fairs and street festivals would be the right place for a signing, since the set

---

8   Editors of Chase's, *Chase's Calendar of Events 2007* ((McGraw-Hill 2007)

up is not conducive for an event. If you are a new author, trying to build up a fan base and recognition, I strongly encourage you to participate in signings at these types of venues.

Then, of course, there are celebrities who only do signings simply because that's all they need to do because of their star status. As a fledgling author, this is not, however, the way to promote yourself.

For example, just recently I was on the roster to do a signing at a local street festival's booth. I was sandwiched between two other authors, all of us given one-hour time slots. The day could not have been any more gorgeous, and people filled the street. When I arrived, the author prior to my signing was sitting at a table, pen in hand, ready to sign copies of his just-released novel. People were strolling by, but I'm not sure if they even saw him and he didn't seem too eager to meet potential book buyers. Finally, it was time for him to pack up, since his time slot was over and mine about to begin. However, I didn't sit in the chair that he offered as he stood to leave. Instead, I took a full-page article that had recently been published about both Susan Isaac's and my novels in *Long Island Woman* magazine and slipped it into a Plexiglas holder, placing it on the table with my books. I then grasped a copy of my novel and stood, attempting to make eye contact with passersby. Within that hour's time, I managed to give out my business cards and sell several copies of my novel. Among the many people I met, one was a librarian, and another a woman who had book discussions in her home. Both women were very interested in doing something with me in support of my novel. But then my hour was up, and the next author came. This well-known author has written several self-help books. I left, but was later told that she had stood back in the booth waiting for people to approach her. As it turns out, among the three authors who did signings that day, I had sold the most books.

The moral? Even if you are doing *only* a signing, make it a "standing" and be ready to greet passersby.

SANTA CLAUS IS COMING TO TOWN!
SHOULD YOU BE?

Even though I believe that events are more advantageous to do than signings, there are times when straight signings make the most sense, no matter who you are.

There are two schools of thought when booking events around the major holidays. Many bookstores block out the time from Thanksgiving through the New Year, limiting the number and type of events they have in their stores. They are focusing on trying to satisfy the busy holiday shoppers and don't want to host any events that might interfere. However, if you have a book that would make a perfect holiday gift, I strongly suggest finding the right venue to have a signing. Why just a signing? Most people are dashing around during the holidays and don't feel that they can take time to sit and listen to a presentation, no matter how fascinating it may be. However, an autographed copy of your book may help those harried shoppers in finding just the right gift for their family and friends.

As long as the venue manager approves, you may want to have some light refreshments available. Food will draw customers to your table, and, while they are munching on a cookie, you will have an opportunity to introduce yourself, your book, and the suggestion of how autographed copies make a unique gift. Be sure to have gift wrap, bows, and tape handy. There's nothing easier than wrapping a book! Also, be prepared in case the customer wants several copies of your autographed book; have Post-it notes handy to identify which autographed book is for whom. Now that is good customer service, directly from the author!

Again, think about your book and the places that would benefit from your doing a signing during the holiday season. If you book meshes with the message of your church or your neighbor's church, see if you could have a signing one evening there. If it's a romance novel, see if you could do a signing at the local lingerie shop. The number of possibilities should excite you!

Take a moment now and write down at least five possible venues that may work for your book. Don't discount an idea simply because it sounds foolish to you. Write the ideas down, begin exploring what you could do for these venues, and then bring the idea as a formal, enthusiastic proposal to their tables.

Chapter 7

NOW WHAT?

You've made sure your press materials are concise and intriguing and had a second and third pair of eyes read everything to be sure there were no errors before you sent it out. You have your calendar open and a pen ready and are waiting for the phone to ring. And you wait. Days go by, and you begin to wonder if the materials had even been received. After all, things do get lost in the mail. It's more likely, however, that yours didn't get lost in the mail, but that it was simply tossed in a pile of unopened mail to be looked at later—at some point. Keep an Excel sheet or some form of record of what you sent out, to whom, and when. After a week's time, call the contact to make sure that your material was received. If it wasn't, ask if you could call back in a few days to follow up. If they agree, then do so. And if the material was still not received, resend it. Chances are, it was received but has been "misplaced."

As an aside, when I am sending out press materials via the United States Postal Service, I spend an extra fifty cents for delivery confirmation. This allows me to track the package using the confirmation number via the USPS Web site (www.usps.com). It saves me time wondering if it had been lost in the mail. The post office also provides priority mail envelopes that you may want to use. Either way, tracking the packages you send will save you time and aggravation.

However, let's say that your information had been received and the contact hadn't yet looked it over. Be polite while asking when would be a good time to follow up, *after* the materials were perused. You don't want to be a nudge, but you ought to be able to say something in the phone call or e-mail that would interest the contact enough to want to look over the press materials.

For instance, when I was trying to get an article with the *Plattsburgh Press Republican* for *Without Grace*, I sent a press kit and followed up with an e-mail, but to no avail. I was scheduled to do an event in upstate New York, not far from where my novel takes place, and I wanted to support the event by promoting it with an article, one I thought would be rather easy to get since I was originally from the area and was now a published author. After a couple of attempts to get the reporter from the paper to respond, I realized that I was competing for stories about an upcoming election. I was scheduled to do an event in early October of 2005, and it was right about the time when the region was mired in a controversy about windmill turbine energy. Some of the locals were adamantly opposed to it and others for it. It was an issue that voters were paying attention to and reporters were writing about.

Even though my novel takes place in the late 1960s, it deals in part with an environmental issue, as well. Therefore, I pitched the idea of my addressing the then *and* now, real *and* fictional environmental issues with the newspaper. It was then that staff writer Suzanne Moore scheduled a time to interview me over the phone, and less than a week before my event there was close to a half-page article titled, "North Country Novel Takes Author Back To Her Roots."[9] And how much of the environmental issue was a part of the article?

There's no Benny's Lake in Churubusco, but the uproar that ensues in *Without Grace* over the proposed development of

---

9   Suzanne Moore, "North Country Novel Takes Author Back to Her Roots," *Press-Republican*, October 30, 2005

that landmark and its environs offers an interesting parallel to real life tumult over wind farms now taking place in Hoenig's hometown.

That was it. The rest of the article was about my novel, my writing, and my having been from the area so many years earlier. The event I did the following week was to a packed house, and I have to believe that that article played an important part in it.

The point is, do not give up; find a way to break through. But be sure to expend your energy on an event that would make sense for all concerned.

It's a Go, Not a No!

The manager or host has received your materials and after playing phone tag, you were able to discuss what you planned to do if she were so kind as to give you a date for the event. By letting her know that you were taking responsibility for the event's success, she eventually agreed to give you a date. It may have been grudgingly, but she did. Congratulations! So, let's figure out what you ought to do now.

First, keep your promise to the venue and get people to attend. Will you be sending out invitations via actual mail, e-mail, or both? And did you mention that you would place an ad in the local paper announcing the event? If so, do it. Your credibility is on the line. Also, communication is the key. You must communicate with your intended audience to entice them to come to your event and you must communicate with your contact at the venue, which is a lesson I learned a long time ago.

As I stated earlier, I was an events coordinator for years for a major bookstore chain, and, for most of those years, I was based out of one particular bookstore in Manhattan. I had the opportunity to work with both small and large publishers and with authors who were just beginning and those with celebrity status. Even so, there was no surefire way of knowing what to expect in way of a turnout. Publicists and authors would call me, trying to get a sense of what they could expect, and I rarely could give them a satisfactory answer—no matter if the author was well-known or not.

As the author, you will need to present a clear plan of what you intend to do while also being flexible. For instance, during your initial communication you will have let the event coordinator, manager, or whoever your contact is for the venue know whether you will be doing just a straight signing or also a reading *and* signing. (I strongly encourage the latter.) Early in my career as an events coordinator, I made a mistake in promoting one particular event. I had written in the store's newsletter and on signage that the author would be doing a reading and discussion, along with the signing. However, when the author appeared that evening, she had been under the impression that she would be sitting at a table and simply signing copies of her book. She hadn't been prepared to read or discuss what she'd written and had clearly been frazzled by the possibility. Staff at the store had taken time to set up chairs and a podium, but the author had wanted nothing to do with it.

I then had to let those who were seated know that a miscommunication had occurred and that the author was only going to sign. Needless to say, there had been disappointment, and no one had bought the book. Unfortunately, both the author and I had appeared unprofessional. This could have been avoided had the author and I discussed ahead of time what she had wanted to do. From that point on, I found out from the author and/or publicist what would be expected and had it in writing. It is amazing how many authors don't realize the difference between an event and a signing, so be clear with the coordinator what you plan to do when you schedule your events *or* signings.

ACTIVATE YOUR EVENT

Either way, whether you are doing just signing or a reading *and* signing, you are hoping for a crowd, as is the host. However, it takes more than hope; it takes time and hard work. (And you thought being a writer was difficult!) Some places require more work than others due to a variety of factors. In Manhattan, for instance, on any given day there are any number of events, author or otherwise. It's a town competing for everyone's attention. Just take a walk in Times Square and see the ubiquitous flashing signs and huge billboards all vying for attention. Oftentimes, it's too much to absorb. Therefore, even if the author is a celebrity, something may throw a monkey wrench in an event's success.

It is here where I must mention the monkey wrench that dramatically hurt events I scheduled during the period of 1996–2001. Whenever then-President Clinton was in New York, the attendance for my events was abysmal. Why? As it happened, the former president always stayed at the Waldorf-Astoria when he was in town, which happened to be a few short blocks from the store where I worked. If the president was being escorted either in or out of Manhattan by his lengthy, traffic-stopping retinue, it clogged the city—at least the city in the ten-block radius from wherever the president was. There were evenings when customers were not the only ones who could not get to the scheduled event but the authors as well because of the traffic. Unfortunately, I just wasn't able to convince the White House to give me the president's schedule so that I would know what dates to avoid when scheduling events! Seriously, though, a few years later I did have an opportunity to work with the president when he was doing signings for his book *My Life,* and he couldn't have been any more gracious.

The point is, be aware of any possible glitches that may affect your event.

PREPARE THE WAY

I don't send out invitations that would require an RSVP for events like those that I had sent for my book launch, which I'll go into detail later, but I do send out e-mail blasts. I previously mentioned my discussion with Debbi Honorof. One of Honorof's suggestions for e-mail blasts is to send blasts to consumers on Fridays but to send to businesses on Mondays. This small bit of information can help get your blast read instead of lost in all the other e-mails that are being received.

One more final comment about e-mail blasts: While they are good to get the word out, a personalized e-mail will be more effective. True, it will take more time to send them, but, if you are reaching out to individuals as opposed to a mass of faceless people, it's quite likely you'll get a better response.

Ideally, the venue will also have a mail list. Chances are they will not be able to give you this list; however, offer to give the venue the invitations that you have prepared. Anything you can do to make their job easier will only benefit you in the long run.

Know Your Way

Once those invitations or announcements have been sent, be sure you know exactly how to get to the location where you will be if you'll be coming in from out of town. (If it's local, I can only shake my head in wonder if you have no idea where it is located, which means you didn't do your homework.) Also, find out from the host if there is usually heavy traffic during the time when you are expected to arrive. You may need to leave earlier than you might think. There is nothing worse than being late for your own event! (Well, granted, there are *many* things worse, but I would avoid it if I were you.)

Fine or Extra Fine?

In addition, something that I did before my book launch, which was my very first event, was go shopping. Did I buy a new dress? Well, yes, but that's not what I'm referring to here. I went pen shopping! I know it sounds silly, since any old pen should do, and they will in a pinch; however, there is something special about owning a pen solely for autographing copies of your book. Some authors like Sharpies, which come in different tips: fine, extra fine, or ultra fine, as well as different colors. I always had a large array of choices when I hosted author events, but every once in awhile an author would arrive with their pen preference in hand. Other times, authors or their publicist would call ahead to let me know what they wanted, and I was expected to have them available. Yes, there was actually a discussion on pen selection, so it's an important topic for every author doing an autographing.

Admittedly, I haven't tested every type of pen, but the one that I presently prefer is the Pilot G2 retractable rolling ball with black gel ink. I always carry several with me, even when I'm not doing an event, since I have actually come across some people who wanted me to sign a copy of my book that they had with them. Hey, it happens—even for a no-name like me!

Is This Thing On?

Ask if the venue has a sound system, table, and chairs. If you are expecting a crowd, a sound system will be important. If the venue doesn't have one available, find out if they will share the cost of renting one with you. If not, plan to speak very loudly or cough up the money to rent your own. However, if you are donating proceeds from the sale of your book to a charity, see if the company will donate the use of the sound system. Be sure to let them know that they will be acknowledged for doing so in any press materials or advertising that you'll be doing.

Try to get an idea of how the room is set up beforehand. If you are not able to drop by the venue due to distance or your schedule, see if there are photos on the Web site. If not, kindly ask the host to send you a picture, or at least a design of the room.

Also, if you have an e-mail list, it would be wise to send out a follow-up reminder. People are busy. They tend not to commit to anything until the day of, so a little reminder from you may be all that they need.

Be sure to stay in touch with the host leading up to the event without being annoying. Make sure that you are doing what you promised, and let the host know as much. The communication will help build confidence with the host and will leave nothing to guesswork. Fortunately, this kind of communication and confidence between one particular author and myself prevented a disaster.

Years ago, I had booked a particular author in support of his book, which was somewhat controversial. We decided that it lent itself to a panel discussion, so we managed to get some weighty names to participate. The day of the event, the author was doing media in Manhattan. He gave me his cell phone number in case any issues arose. As it happened, about three hours before the event was scheduled, a bookseller paged me and said that the author had called the store to cancel the event. By this time, I had rented one hundred chairs and extra microphones, and the staff was in the process of setting everything up. They wanted to know if they should dismantle it all.

However, that phone call appeared fishy to me, since the author had always called my direct line when we needed to go over details. Before telling the staff it was canceled, I called the author's cell phone, and, sure enough, he hadn't called the store. He did tell me that some people didn't want him to do the event, so he was sure that one of them had made the call.

Happily, the panel discussion went as planned and we had a full house and sold many copies of the book.

Introduction

The point is, stay in communication with the host in order to avoid any possible snafus. You will also need to know if the host normally introduces the author or if you will need to wing it on your own. I have been introduced at some of my events, and at others I have introduced myself. Either way worked for me since I was prepared. So be prepared to introduce yourself, even if the host said that they will do so. Situations sometimes arise, and the host may suddenly be nowhere to be found when you need to begin.

Also, find out if the host or someone else will be assigned to assist you. Preferably, you want someone on hand to help if the sound system fails or if there is a disgruntled guest in attendance. If the venue doesn't plan to schedule an assistant, try to bring a friend along, someone who is willing to chat up the crowd, get you water or be the one to introduce you. This friend may be helpful also by telling the audience that the author needs to wrap the event up. This way, the author is not the bad guy, leaving the impression that he or she is unwilling to spend time with those in attendance.

When I do events, my "assistant," who is also my very good friend, Peggy, comes along to help me. Peggy has traveled all the way to upstate New York in the winter with me for a number of events and helps with the sales of my book. And, as if that weren't enough, she has even drove me from Long Island to Savannah, Georgia, to attend a book discussion based on my novel. While I focus on my presentations, Peggy schmoozes with the guests. In that schmoozing, she also makes contacts for future events, and the cycle is repeated. Every author should have a Peggy in his or her life. Besides, we have the best time on our road trips. I'm a horrible navigator, but I do a pretty good job playing dj.

Decide Your Presentation

Only a few days ago I participated on a panel with several other writers. We were told well ahead of time that each of us would have approximately five minutes for our own presentations. Bearing that in mind, I wrote up the points I wanted to address to the audience and timed myself. I clocked my talk to be just under five and a half minutes long and I read it aloud several times in preparation.

The day of the discussion, the host introduced the first author, who spoke for about fifteen minutes. She seemed to have a lot of territory she wanted to cover and tried to fit it all in, while making no specific point. Several other authors were introduced; some had good presentations while others were lacking. One author in particular actually appeared to have been caught off guard when asked to speak. When it was my turn, I knew what I planned to say, did so, and appreciated the enthusiastic response when I concluded. At the end of the discussion, we were all given an opportunity to sell our books, and I couldn't help but notice the difference in book sales between a clear and concise presentation and one that rambles.

I would also like to offer some advice to any author who is on a panel. If there has been a time limit put on your presentation, as there must be, adhere to it—especially if you are sharing the podium with others. Even though you may believe what you have to say is fascinating and merits more time, going over the time limit is rude not only to your counterparts on the panel, but to the audience who is hoping to have time to ask questions.

SELL YOURSELF

Remember why you are doing events in the first place: to sell books. You do want to sell books, don't you? I just heard you yell, "Of course I do, you idiot!"

Then *you* must be your own salesperson. When it comes to the point where it's just you and your audience, this is your time to shine. Your book got you there, but now you must be prepared to sell it. No longer is it about the publisher, the publicist, or even the venue; now it is about *you.*

Like I stated earlier, the events I used to book felt like a revolving door of authors. There was little variety of what would transpire. I was always amazed at how many of these authors would ask me before they walked in front of their audience, no matter the size, "What did you want me to talk about?"

I have a somewhat acerbic tongue and was often tempted to let it speak my mind; however, I usually suggested that the author read from or talk about his or her book. It was then I knew that the "event" was going to be less than exciting. Imagine attending an event where the author hadn't prepared. Would you be likely to buy his or her book?

Your John Hancock

You've bought the pens; now think, too, about what you might want to use as your signature in books, if it's going to be personalized. For my book launch, I tended to write something personal and different for all my guests, since they were friends and business associates, but for events where I do not know the people, I tend to keep it simple. Some of the dedications I use are, "Enjoy!" "Happy reading!" "Thanks for your support!" I also make sure that the customer spells his or her name for me. Or, if there is a long line, you may want to have your assistant go through the line with Post-it notes and clearly write out the names so that you are able to see the actual spelling. There are a number of ways to spell Christine. Or Kristine. Or Cristine. Or—well, you get my point.

Checklist

So, now that you are ready to bring your book to the masses, please consider the following for each event:

- Who will be my audience?

- What portion of my book will apply to this specific audience?

- How long will I be expected to speak?

- Will there be an opportunity for Q&A?

- Will I be able to handle any possible question coming from the audience?

- Have I rehearsed?

- Whom do I need to thank formally either before or after my talk?

- Are there any upcoming holidays or events in which I need to remind the audience that an autographed book would make a great gift?

KNOW WHERE YOU ARE

This may seem like a foolish statement, but you must be aware of where you are speaking and why you have been invited. For instance, within a week's time, I spoke to a local branch of the American Association of University Women, to students at my old high school, and to a large audience in a bookstore. Weeks before I went to speak to members of the AAUW, I researched the organization online and discovered their interests, as well as their mission statement. I spoke to the woman who had invited me and confirmed how long I was to talk and what to expect. I also arranged to have books available for sale by contacting the local bookstore in the area well ahead of time. They agreed to attend the event with the books, cash drawer, and credit card machine, which are important details, since you want to meet your customers' needs while not missing any possible sales.

On the day of the event, I arrived twenty minutes before my scheduled time to speak and mingled with the women until it was time for me to approach the podium. Although I often tend to fail at placing names with faces, I tried to remember the names of some of the women I'd met during our informal chat. After I was formally introduced, I thanked the group for having invited me and then read a couple of paragraphs from my novel. Then I spoke on the topic of being both a woman and a struggling writer. Once I finished, I took questions, making certain to recognize the names of some of the women who had their hands raised. Before I closed, I thanked everyone who had taken the time to hear me speak and also reminded them that both Hanukkah and Christmas was approaching and that a personally autographed copy of my book would make a nice gift. Someone in the audience always responds to that and buys at least one copy for someone as a gift. When I walked away from the podium, there was already a line to have me sign copies of my book.

Days later, I was standing in front of the students from my alma mater, but very little of what I had said at the American Association of University Women would be of much interest to my adolescent audience. I had also previously arranged to have a local bookstore about thirty miles from the school bring copies of my novel to sell. It was a cold winter day, so I was grateful that the store was willing to go offsite.

The grades ranged from seventh to twelfth, and each class was brought in to the auditorium during their English period. Once it was established what grade I was speaking to, I geared myself accordingly. However, I was prepared, knowing that I would be speaking to students—fidgety, restless students. I read a small portion from my book, which wasn't the same portion I'd read to the AAUW, talked some about what it had been like years ago when I had attended the very school where they were students, and then immediately opened the floor to questions. A number of hands shot up. The questions ranged from "How long have you been writing?" to "Did you know my Mom?"

I didn't just stand in front of the class. I walked around and asked the young girls and boys about their interests. I also mentioned some of the surnames from the area that I used in my novel. That day, I sold a large quantity of books.

A couple of days later, I did an event at the local bookstore in the area, the same bookstore that came to the school to sell copies. There were about fifty people in attendance, many who were curious as to how I had turned out after having moved away thirty years earlier. I purposely read a specific portion from the novel that dealt with an environmental issue. I figured that since the region was going through a very real environmental issue at the time, one that was making news on a daily basis, it would be an interesting aspect of my book. My audience was riveted, even though my story took place much earlier than what was currently happening in the region. Once I finished reading, I was prepared to be pulled into the polemical discussion, but, as it happens, I was asked more about my life as a writer. Apparently, my audience wanted a reprieve from the controversy, and, shifting gears, I gave it to them.

As I had with the women from AAUW and the students, I invited everyone at the event to stay in touch with me, and I gave them my contact information to do so. As it happens, I was invited to return to my high school a few months later for the school's Literary Café. Since I had managed to sell quite a few copies of my novel the first time, the bookstore was more than willing to send someone with more books to sell a second time around. In addition, a local chapter of AAUW has invited me to speak at their Book and Author Luncheon in the spring of 2007, and I've already contacted the local bookstore to mark their calendar in order to attend and sell copies of my book for me.

Joanne and Martha, friends from my high school days, stopped by to say hello.

Writer, interviewer, and now good friend, Gordie Little.

Veronica Franklin, my English teacher, attended my book event.

Meeting students and staff at my old alma mater.

Invited back to my alma mater.

Chapter 8

═══════════════════════

IT'S HEEEERE ...

It's the day of your event, and you've left nothing to chance. Your main concern is whether you are going to have two or two hundred people in attendance. Is there any way to gauge it?

Not really.

Unlike a book launch where you would want to have your invited guests RSVP so that you are prepared with the right amount of food, beverages, and those all-important books, events are not quite so easy to figure out. So you must first ask yourself a tough question.

WHAT MAKES A SUCCESSFUL EVENT?

The question merits a response, but it's one you, the author, must answer. If Stephen King had twelve people show up at his book signing, that is a debacle; if you or I had twelve people for an event for our first published book, I'd say that was successful. I have done events, as well as hosted some, where only two people have attended. As far as I'm concerned, those events were not a failure. Instead, I looked at it as an opportunity to sit and chat with the two people who took the time to show up to hear me read and discuss my book. In other words, I was building my fan base. I also look at it as the ripple effect.

If I had walked out visibly annoyed at who *didn't* show up, the two who were there would have witnessed an author who didn't care that they had taken time out of their schedule to come. Instead, I pulled up a chair, chatted with the women, and ended up selling three books. (One bought a copy for a friend who had wanted to come but couldn't make it.) Hopefully, those two women told others about the intimate conversation we had, and word of mouth is often the best advertiser—especially when the words are positive!

Conversely, I've hosted authors who have done quite the opposite. One author in particular comes to mind. He was a household name for a couple of decades and was going to do a signing in my store (notice that I said *signing*). I had enough co-op from the publisher to take out an ad in the newspaper. I also splashed posters throughout the store promoting the upcoming signing. I sent out press releases to the media contact list I thought might be interested. I had the staff talk it up to customers. I kept in contact with the author's manager on a daily basis. To keep the expected crowd control in line, I had the store set up stanchions and assigned extra staff to help. Clearly, I was expecting a crowd of excited fans.

To my chagrin, thirty minutes before the event, no one had yet showed up. The author was in his hotel a couple of blocks away with the manager, who called to see how things were going. I had to be honest and tell him that no one had shown up yet. However, I did mention that the store was notorious for people arriving at the last minute, which was true. I hoped it would be the case for this particular event.

About fifteen minutes before the signing was to start, I had five people standing in line. These were five excited people, eager to meet the author. About the same time, the manager showed up *without* the author. He was none too happy with the small turnout. I gave him the event folder with all the copies of press releases I'd sent, ads I'd run, and so forth, so that he would not have me to blame. Trust me, there is a lot of finger-pointing when an author event is not deemed successful, but it's rarely pointed at the author. I also explained that those who had shown up were galvanized and would provide energy that could hopefully build into a crowd. He then left to go back to get the author. Or so he said.

Once the scheduled time came for the signing to begin, there were about twelve people in line, all waiting to have their book signed, some with more than one copy. Unfortunately, the manager called me from his cell phone saying that the author was stuck in his limousine with a flat tire on the Long Island Expressway and would not be able to make the signing. Of course, I knew that was not the case, because just moments before he had been a few short blocks away, while the LIE is miles from the store. However, I had to break the bad news to the twelve people in line. None were too happy, and all but two returned their purchases.

As I said, this author had been a household name. Would more people have shown up had he done an actual event instead of just a signing? It is quite likely. Even if it the attendance had doubled, it would have been a nice gathering. It's quite likely, though, that the location wasn't ideal but had been selected for the author's convenience. I'm not sure what he's doing now, but not having a crowd should not be reason enough not to appreciate those who do show up—no matter who you are.

Therefore, whether you have two or two hundred, give the people who took the time to show up 100 percent. They'll remember that for a long, long time, and that makes a successful event.

MAKE A GOOD FIRST IMPRESSION

It's the day of the event. Whether you have traveled a great distance or are just walking down the block, you need to be mentally and physically prepared.

Let's say you've written an authoritative book on wine tasting. It's an attractive book with a glossy cover. It's an eye-catcher. Because of these things, you have no doubt that it will sell. Unfortunately, your event is about to begin, and you had given little thought to what you were going to wear and whether you should have gotten a haircut and a manicure.

Sure, it's about the book, but, as your book's representative, you must present yourself worthy.

First, let me say this: I love C-SPAN Book TV. Weekends are better because of the forty-eight-hour programming that it offers. (If only I could convince my friends at Book TV to give some airtime to fiction!) Sometimes I find myself drawn in to the subject matter, and other times I find myself cringing at the author who appears to have just climbed out of bed. The suit is crumpled and the hair uncombed. The author may be offering some profound information, but I am not paying attention. If he didn't think his message was worth dressing up for, I automatically suppose he's right. I cannot help but wonder, did no one tell him he was going to be on national television?

Television or not, if you are doing an event, take some time to physically prepare yourself. Make sure your clothes are clean—don't laugh, I've hosted authors whose shirt announced what they had for dinner—and make sure your outfit is pressed. Look in a mirror prior to speaking and take a closer look at your teeth to make sure remnants of your spinach salad aren't still there.

Having a professional appearance will give you credibility, and your audience will be more likely to pay attention to your message instead of to a slovenly appearance.

Fashionably Late Is Unfashionably Rude

Arrive on time, but do not start on time. Wait five to ten minutes for stragglers, because there will always be stragglers. Use the time to check the sound system, if there is a sound system, and to make sure you have your beverage of choice within reach from where you will be speaking. You can also approach those who arrived on time and thank them for coming. This would be a good moment to ask how they had heard about the event, which is a question I always ask. It helps me to know which types of promotion work and which don't.

Whether you've been introduced by the host or have introduced yourself, do not follow that introduction by instantly putting your head down and reading from your book. Take time to thank everyone for coming and hold your book up (your own copy that you brought with you) to let them know how excited you are to have an opportunity to share it with them. Again, it's about passion, and you want everyone in attendance to see just how passionate you are about your topic so that they will be inspired to buy what you are selling: your book! However, your passion should not be long-winded. Keep your presentation to no more than thirty minutes. Once you have finished, you should then open the floor to your audience for questions or comments. Be prepared, because no matter whether you wrote a book about a serious topic or a fantasy novel, here are some questions you can expect:

1. What inspired you to write your book?

2. When do you usually write?

3. What are you working on now?

4. Was it difficult to find a publisher?

5. Are you married?

6. Do you have children?

7. What does your family think about this book?

8. I have a book I started. Would you mind taking a look at it? I just know that people would want to buy it.

9. How long have you been writing?

10. I am a big fan of Brigitte Bardot, and I think someone should write a book about her. Would you be able to do that?

Don't laugh at that last one. When I hosted events for the bookstore, there was always one particular customer who came to every single event. She never bought a book, but she did ask every author who spoke if they would consider writing a book about the French actress. I always fore-warned the authors about this particular quirky audience member and usually found their response to her rather amusing, especially since they had been prepared that the question may arise. Finally, after a couple of weeks of this customer's persistence, I had to intervene and suggest that, since she was such a fan, perhaps she could write a book about Bardot. Unfortunately, she didn't find the idea very helpful.

What this story shows, though, is that an author needs to be prepared for just about anything. If you are doing an event in a bookstore setting, anyone can sit in one of the chairs set up for the event, whether the person is there for you or just to stay inside from the cold. I have even had to ask customers to move from the table that was set up for the author while the author stood waiting to begin. Sometimes the customer would give me an insolent look and say, "Now?"

"Yes, now."

This is one reason why doing events for corporations and the like, as Kim Ricketts arranges, oftentimes avoids those awkward situations. But, invariably, there will be awkward situations, and you will need to learn to go with the flow.

DON'T WEAR OUT YOUR WELCOME

Perhaps you have nothing to do for the rest of the evening and are having a great time talking with audience members, but that does not mean your host doesn't have anything else to do. Learn to keep your events within the timeframe previously discussed with the host. Close by thanking everyone once again and reminding them that your book is for sale and that you will be signing copies. If you are giving a percentage to a special cause, be sure to tell them that, as well. And, of course, remind everyone that an autographed copy of your book would make a great gift for an upcoming holiday or special occasion. An additional idea is to have a notebook where customers can leave their e-mail addresses. Let them know that you would be happy to keep them posted on upcoming events and other publications you are doing.

There may be a few stragglers who still want to talk with you, so you or your assistant will need to make it clear that the event has concluded. Be sure to thank your host personally and let them know that you would be happy to return in the future.

CHECKLIST

Here is an event checklist for you to look over as a quick guide.

After the event has been confirmed, be sure to do the following:

1. One month prior to the event, send out an e-mail blast and be sure to give your host a copy to send to their mail list.

2. One month prior to the event, confirm all the details for the event (travel time, room setup, etc.).

3. A week in advance, contact the host again to be sure everything is as scheduled.

4. Three days in advance, send out a follow-up e-mail to your list, reminding them of your event.

5. Three days in advance, prepare your introduction.

The day of the event, be sure to do the following:

1. Look presentable.

2. Bring your copy of your book, pens, business cards, and notepad.

3. Check your teeth for any food and clothes for opened buttons and zippers.

4. Arrive early.

5. Introduce yourself to your host and those who have already arrived. (You may want to ask them to fill out the notepad with their contact information, if they so choose.)

6. Prepare your beverage of choice to bring to the podium.

7. Check that the sound system is on and working, if there is one.

While you're at the podium, be sure to do the following:

1. Thank everyone for coming and hold up your book so that the cover is visible.

2. Look at your audience and tell them that you will be autographing copies at the end of your presentation.

3. Let the audience know that, after your presentation, you will open the floor for questions.

4. Stand tall and with confidence. (Remember you are selling a product.)

5. Don't rush your words or keep looking at your watch.

6. Open the floor for questions once you have finished your talk.

7. Put a limit on your talk in order to give yourself time to sign books.

8. Be prepared for any possible comment or question.

9. Thank everyone and let them know where you'll be signing books.

10. Remind your audience that an autographed copy of a book makes a great gift.

11. Do not sign the book without first hearing how the person's name is spelled.

12. Find the host and thank them for their time and effort.

Chapter 9

═══════════════════

MAINTAINING MOMENTUM

As you have most certainly gathered by now, being an author is much more than simply writing a book. It takes hard work, stamina, and perseverance. It also takes creative thinking. Earlier, I referenced some publications that addressed this very topic, but recently I came across an article that was published in the *Miami Herald* in the business section. The headline read: "For authors, writing's just half the job. In today's multimedia world, authors must leave no stone unturned in marketing their books."[10]

Business book critic Richard Pachter, who wrote the article, confirmed everything I've been telling you. But his last paragraph, quoting writer Seth Godin, was the clincher:

> His advice to authors is to get out and really work for their books: "You need a platform to make a published book work. If you don't have a platform yet, you should self-publish your first book and give away enough copies to get a platform, and then use that platform to engage your readers so that you can sell the second one to a publisher and quit your day job."

---

10   Richard Pachter, "For Authors, Writing's Just Half the Job," *Miami Herald*, November 14, 2006

CREATURES OF HABIT

I used to be surprised when dealing with publicists from traditional publishing houses. It often felt as though they dealt with each author in similar fashion, unless, of course the author was of celebrity status. That's when all the stops were pulled. I was often frustrated by this, since the midlist authors tend to be the ones who are building a fan base and coming out with another book every few years, even though they haven't yet reached the sales to be on the *New York Times* bestseller list. In other words, a midlist author is someone who is well received but hasn't had a commercial breakthrough. When I was hosting events for the midlist author, the publicist was allotted a certain amount of dollars to promote the event. However, it was usually the same publicity campaign for each author. Very little was done to nurture these authors' careers.

If the author was scheduled to do an event in one of my stores, I would offer promotional ideas to make it more than just an event, but my ideas were usually discouraged by the publicist, since their budget was already allocated. Therefore, each store was given enough money to make flyers or posters announcing the event. And that was it. Creative, huh? Posters and flyers are important, but identifying the author's audience would have been wiser, and, in turn, investing more money to that constituency would have been smarter. Unfortunately, many publicists do not have the time to think creatively so they do what has been done for years and hope for the best.

The good news for you is that you are receiving the tools to power up your career without wasting your valuable time and money.

Now that you know how to do an event, what's next?

AFTER THE EVENT

It's never really over, not if you want to build up that fan base. The day after your event, even though you've already thanked the host, send a personal thank-you note. This will also give you the opportunity to offer to do another event in the future if you felt it was worth the time and energy, but it will also show that you value the host's time. In addition, you may ask the host if he or she would be willing to write an endorsement that could be used for future events elsewhere. That said, ask the host what he or she feels you could have done to improve the overall presentation, if he or she had been present. Let the host know that any suggestions will only add to your next event. Also, if the host receives any comments from those who attended, ask if he or she could pass them on to you. Be sure to tell them that you don't need to know who said what, but would appreciate the feedback for future reference.

Also, take the list of e-mail addresses that you managed to collect at the event and e-mail each person, thanking them for taking the time to attend. Ask them, too, what they enjoyed about the presentation and what they felt was lacking. If you receive a response that could be used as a blurb for future promotion, get permission from the person before using it.

Now sit back and think about the event from your vantage point. How did you feel it went? Nothing is flawless, so there must have been something you felt could be improved for the next time. Perhaps the portion of the book you read didn't connect with the audience. Maybe you shouldn't read at all but should just talk about your book and what inspired you to write it. Or perhaps your talk was continuously interrupted by the whooshing sound of a nearby espresso machine drowning out your words. Shouting at your audience does seem a bit unprofessional. Next time, waiting for the machine to stop would probably work to your advantage. What about that one audience member who kept hogging the conversation; were you able to gently give attention elsewhere without insulting him or her? Will you be able to do so in the future? Was there someone being aggressively contrary to what you were saying? If so, how did you handle their aggression?

Each event offers another opportunity to improve from your last. Oftentimes, we cannot possibly imagine what will happen, but the sharper we are and the better prepared, we can come out looking professional, thereby giving credibility to our subject.

Chapter 10

===========

YOUR BOOK LAUNCH

Now that you are better prepared to do events, let's consider what your very first event should entail. Since you've worked so hard—from writing your book to getting it published—how about a celebration? This is where the book launch comes in. I like the word *launch* because it implies that you are ready to release your book to the public in celebratory fashion. It's not going to be a typical book event but instead something above and beyond. You will probably need to spend some money to make it a real celebration, but doesn't your book deserve it? Don't *you* deserve it? I know I certainly did.

TIME TO CELEBRATE

When my novel, *Without Grace*, was about to be published, I immediately envisioned a book launch. (Oh, who am I kidding? I envisioned a book launch long before *Without Grace* was going to be published!) Since I am on the advisory council for The New York Center for Independent Publishing (formerly called the Small Press Center) in Manhattan, which is housed in the landmark building of the General Society of Mechanics and Tradesmen, I couldn't think of a better place to have the celebration. Tucked between Fifth and Sixth Avenues, the building is in the heart of Literary Row, where the *New Yorker* once was and where the Roundtable gang gathered to talk about a number of topics—most notably, writing. Actually, the famous Algonquin Hotel is just a short walk down 44th Street from The New York Center for Independent Publishing.

I envisioned guests walking down the set of stairs that open up into a main reading room where books fill long rows of shelves. If the guests looked up, they would discover the magnificent skylight three stories high. I couldn't think of a better place to introduce my novel to family, friends, and business associates.

Therefore, once I was given a publication date for my novel, I didn't waste a moment to book the room. Then I went through my Rolodex, stacks of business cards, e-mail list, and address book and began to alphabetically enter all the contact information on an Excel sheet. (A word to the wise: This is something you will want to do long before you get a publication date. It will also not only be a timesaver but a confirmation that you believe in yourself and deserve to celebrate what you've accomplished.)

To handle the sale of my book, I arranged to have a bookseller present. This way I didn't have to handle money and take time away from mingling with my guests.

I knew the date would be busy for many of those on my guest list since it was in the fall, which is during a time of book launches all over the city. Therefore, I sent out an early e-mail letting people know that I was planning to celebrate the release of my book. In the subject line, I wrote: "Carol Hoenig Would Like For You To Hold The Date!" I sent the e-mail out on July 14. Here is what the actual e-mail said:

September 20th, 2005 at 6 PM—Hold this date and time!

(A formal e-vitation to come.)

Celebrate the book launch for
Without Grace by Carol Hoenig
at The Small Press Center
20 West 44th St. (Between 5th & 6th Aves.)

I also had a brief bio and included the blurbs I had managed to acquire.

With the teaser, I received about twenty RSVPs. On August 23, I then sent out the e-vitation:

Please join Carol Hoenig in celebration of the publication of her novel
When: Tuesday, September 20th, 6 PM–8:30 PM
Where: Small Press Center at 20 West 44th Street (Btw 5th & 6th)
Light refreshments will be served.

Please RSVP by September 10th
To: <u>carolhoenig@carolhoenig.com</u>
Or: (516) XXX-XXXX

What's a party without food and drink? I interviewed some caterers and finally settled on one. We went over the menu and stayed in touch working out the details while I waited for the RSVPs from the long list of invited guests. The evening was not cheap for me, but it was important that the one hundred or so guests knew that I cherished their time. I served soft drinks and wine and had a variety of hors d'oeuvres passed by a wait staff. However, don't feel as though you need to spend thousands of dollars to fete your guests. A sparkling punch with some cookies can do just as well in a pinch.

For the launch, I didn't do a reading or discussion but gave a brief talk thanking everyone for their support and for taking the time to come. I then spent most of the evening signing copies of my novel. To my satisfaction, what I had envisioned actually occurred—well, except for one minor detail. The people I had scheduled to serve the beverages and hors d'oeuvres canceled on me the day before the launch. Admittedly, I had a meltdown. Fortunately, my daughters and son rallied their troops, as well as pitched in, and none of the guests was the wiser. I also managed to get some press, which was difficult to do for a first-time novel by an unknown writer, especially in Manhattan.

From the September 29, 2005, issue of the *New York Sun*:[11]

GRACEFUL PARTY As an events coordinator for Borders, Carol Hoenig is used to assembling crowds for others. But in the library of the General Society of Mechanics and Tradesmen, friends had gathered to celebrate her own novel, "Without Grace," (iUniverse), about a daughter's search for a mother who abandoned her family. Seen were Carmine DeSena, co-author of "The Air Down Here: True Tales from a South Bronx Boyhood" (Chronicle Books); Newmarket Press president Esther Margolis; Philip Rose, author of "You Can't Do That on Broadway" (Limelight Editions); movie producer Sue Pollock; ethnomusicologist Henrietta Yurchenco, author of "Around the World in 80 Years" (Music Research Institute).

---

11   Gary Shapiro, "Graceful Party," *New York Sun*, September 29, 2005

Getting a notice in a New York City paper was worth the couple thousand dollars I'd spent on the food and drink; however, remember, you can give yourself a party rather inexpensively or with even more bells and whistles. It all depends on your time and finances.

My children, Jason, Natasha, and Corrie.
(They waited a long time for this!)

Nicky, Lisa, and Cathy—Forever friends.

Writer and good friend Carmine DeSena introduces me.

The Hair Effex team came to celebrate (and check my coiffure!)

Friend P. J. Campbell, always supportive and encouraging.

Celebrating *Without Grace.*

MORE LAUNCHES

Following are some varied experiences of other authors who celebrated the publication of their books with a launch. What you will see is the uniqueness of each. While reading, consider what you could do to launch your book.

In the fall of 2002, Candlewick Press, a publisher based out of Massachusetts, published *Fairie-ality*, an eye-catching coffee table book. The book is a fashion collection from the House of Ellwand for those whimsical, winged creatures known as fairies! Every page in this book presents unique fashions made from feathers, bark, and other forest finds. Shoes were a big item in the book, so Candlewick Press held a book launch at Stuart Weitzman, a designer shoe store in Manhattan. The creators of *Fairie-ality*, Eugenie Bird, David Downton, and David Ellwand, created a window display incorporating the fairy shoes they'd designed for the book. Using flower petals, birch bark, and pheasant feathers, among other woodland wonders, the shoes were a showstopper even before the guests entered the store.

The evening continued in a most magical way with a harpist plucking the strings of her instrument and a wait staff fluttering by with trays of fanciful hors d'oeuvres. There were no formal introductions or speeches from the creators of this book; instead, they mingled with the guests and thanked each one individually for coming. This party occurred over four years ago, and I still recall it in detail. The creativity of this launch garnered attention for this book, but what did the shoe store gain from it?

In a word: media. Even though the book, too, got some press from the event, the store was mentioned in each write-up. Free press cannot be beat! Also, those fairy shoes in the window encouraged curious shoppers to come inside.

Shooting Water: A Memoir of Second Chances, Family and Filmmaking by Devyani Saltzman was published by Newmarket Press in the spring of 2006. Much of the book's setting is in India and about the Indian culture. Therefore, instead of having a traditional book signing in a bookstore, the author had a book launch at the Indo-American Arts Council. Wine was served, and it was standing room only as Saltzman read some select passages from her book. She also showed a clip from Deepa Mehta's film *Water*. Mehta, who is the author's mother, was also in attendance and added to the excitement. Cameras were flashing, and a lengthy line of guests waited to buy the book. There was also press about both the book and what the Indo-American Arts Council does. It served the council well to host this event.

There are so many other possibilities to build excitement for your book, and first-time novelist S. H. Post, author of *samsara moon* (Kirk House Publishers), has tapped into one. Earlier, you read how this author had a strategy and implemented it to success.

Although he is not yet a celebrity, Post, who is from Long Island, New York, decided to give himself a party in celebration of having written a historical saga. Just like a brand-new ship setting sail, Post wanted to launch his novel into the hands of readers by giving it an encouraging send off. Instead of having just one book party, he pulled off four scattered across the country, while using a fundraiser to support and promote the launch.

Once you have launched your book, it does not mean that the party is over. There are many ways to continue the momentum for promoting your book. But first, let's recap part two by going over the checklist.

RECAPPING PART TWO

- Prepare press kits.

- Use delivery confirmation when sending out press kits.

- Make savvy decisions about when, where, and even if as you consider event venues.

- Respect the manager or host's time when querying him or her.

- Stay in communication with your host for all the details.

- Send e-mail blasts to consumers on Fridays and to businesses on Mondays.

- Go over the event checklist to be sure every event detail is covered.

- Follow up after the event for input.

- Read over the recaps in part 1.

Part 3

TIPS AND TECHNIQUES

Chapter 11

BECOMING A PRO

At this point, my hope is that you not only have a better understanding of how to get your book into customers' hands but the expertise to do so. If you are feeling daunted, let me remind you of the time you took to write your book. Realize that your book is an investment that needs to be compounded by positive aggression. This part of the book will offer some tips and techniques that you may implement to keep the momentum going for your book. It will also provide stories from authors who have found ways to build their fan base.

CONFUSED AND OVERWHELMED

Besides being a writer, I am a publishing consultant, and invariably I am told by authors once their books are published that they have little idea what to do next. How do I get interviews? How do I get a book review? What do I need to do to get an event? Many of these same people have also told me on a number of occasions, "I'm a writer, not a public speaker." Then they tell me how they'll be happy to sit safely behind a table and sign copies of their books.

My response?

Unless you are Madonna, you should do an event as opposed to only a signing. It is smart business. Some people are better at this than others are, but your future fans will come to hear what you have to say. You don't want to lose them. Hiding behind a table is not the way to go about it. Remember, instead of just a straight signing, it often makes more sense to do an event. Repeat after me: "I must do events. I must do events."

PRACTICE, PRACTICE, PRACTICE

The first time you do an event, you will no doubt be nervous. Will you stumble? Will they laugh at you? Quite likely, no, because you will be prepared. Here is how:

Practice what you will say by repeating it aloud to either a friend or family member, or even to yourself prior to the event. Even though you've written the book, you will still need to refresh your memory. Besides, this will give you confidence. And, during the event, do not speak or read sitting down. Your posture will suggest your self-assurance in your material and in yourself. Stand tall and emote. Every so often, if you are reading from a speech or your book, look away from the page and make eye contact with your audience. Smile, if you can multitask! During your talk, ask your audience questions. This came in particularly handy for me some time ago when I was moderating a panel discussion with several authors for a writers' conference.

I was prepared with a long line of questions, but I also had a sheet of paper to jot down questions that were inspired by the immediate conversation. As it happens, my panelists were less than forthcoming and were certainly not chatty, so there was no immediate conversation. Granted, we were the last panel of the day and everyone was a bit exhausted, but, with more than an hour left, I needed to maintain the momentum from the day. Therefore, I turned to the audience and asked if any of them had experienced what I had just asked one of the panelists. Hands shot up, and, immediately, the discussion was saved and it seemed to have sparked the panelists back to life. Therefore, getting your audience involved will bring your book to life. Some of you who are reading this will say under your breath, "I just cannot talk about myself. I am not comfortable doing so. I'm a writer not a public speaker." As your book's biggest proponent, you must get comfortable with the idea.

FOR THE RETICENT AUTHOR

Some people have a lot to say and it's worth hearing, but, unfortunately, they do not have the courage or will to stand in front of people and talk. These people are very content sitting in the privacy of their home at their computers and writing their books. But, horror of horrors, they now need to get out and sell it!

Does this describe you?

If so, let's consider some helpful hints to make it easier for you. Why not find someone who could interview you as part of your event? You will not be alone in front of the audience, and your interviewer will not only act as your buffer but will be able to support you. Most regions have local radio or television hosts who are interested in interviewing authors, even outside of the studio.

For instance, Long Island's radio and television talk show host Larry Davidson is the king of interviewers. He is one of the few who actually reads the books and researches the authors who will be on any one of his programs. Besides interviewing authors on *WGBB Tonite* and local cable's *Davidson & Co.*, Larry does a summer author series at Palmer Vineyards on eastern Long Island. He has been doing this for quite some time, and the series has become more popular each passing year. There is a built-in audience, and, with the vista of vineyards in the background from the porch that serves as a generous space, Larry says "the setting itself has cache."

Each Sunday during the summer months, authors join Larry to discuss their books and take questions from the audience. The interview format helps validate the authors and provides a comfort zone for both authors who may be shy and members in the audience hesitant to ask a question. A local bookstore brings the books to sell onsite, which is another reminder that there are a number of possible locations to sell your book.

But, you say, you don't live on Long Island and cannot get Larry to interview you. That's okay, because you are a creative person. You wrote a book, after all, didn't you? So think creatively. I'll help.

Do you have a friend who is not shy, a friend who would be willing to interview you as part of your event? The two of you could prepare a loose script and work on the questions without sounding too staged. Even if your friend is an unknown name, the event could be promoted thusly:

> Join Jane Doe (your friend) as she discusses John Smith's (you are John Smith) book, *Why I'm Afraid To Speak In Public* (working title), at Madison Square Garden (hey, stranger things have happened) on February 31st (I know, I know). Include in the promotional materials: Jane Doe is a huge fan of John Smith and is eager to ask the author about his book, *Why I'm Afraid To Speak In Public,* and why he wrote it. Questions from the audience will follow the formal discussion.

Okay, so let's say that even though all of your friends love your book, they, too, are extremely shy and would prefer to have root canal than sit in front of an audience interviewing you. No, it's not necessarily time to get new friends. However, if you are in a writers' group, perhaps you could ask a fellow writer to do the honors. You could in turn promise to do the same once his or her book has been published.

Another strong possibility is to contact a journalism class at the local college to see if there would be any students interested in the experience of interviewing a real-life author in front of a real-life audience. Besides the fact that the student/interviewer would get a free copy of the book well in advance in order to prepare, the student would also be able to add the gig to his or her resume. Better yet, perhaps the professor of the journalism course would encourage the rest of the students to take a class trip to your event to support the novice interviewer. The built-in audience would create a buzz. You would also have another angle to pitch to the media about how an author is helping a student on his or her career path in journalism. You would need to allow yourself ample time to arrange this, but it would be well worth it.

GOING SOLO

Let's say that for any number of reasons that you are unable to find someone to interview you for your book events, but you still want to bring your book to an audience. You may want to invest in a media trainer or take a public speaking class. The confidence gained from this will mean the difference between successfully marketing your book or watching it sit lifelessly.

TAKE PASSION TO THE PODIUM

The point is, be prepared to approach your topic in any number of ways, but the one constant that must always maintain is your passion. It will be infectious and might even inspire sales. However, if the passion is missing, the sales may be as well.

Several years ago, during a time when I had decided that I wanted to have a career as a writer while having little idea how to go about it, I had decided to educate myself in a number of ways. One such way had been attending a literary tea in Manhattan at a posh hotel where several authors were speaking. I had been more than excited about one particular author who was scheduled to be on the panel. I had been reading her novels for years and considered her writing to be the best of the best. I had been eager to hear what gems would come from her talk.

The tea had been held in an elegant ballroom, and every table had been filled. Once the author I had been waiting to hear was introduced, she had walked up to the podium, opened her novel, and read without emotion or inflection. She hadn't looked up at the crowd but had continued to read for several minutes before closing her book and walking back to her seat. The applause had been generous because of who she was, but I had been disappointed.

The next author had been introduced, someone whose name I barely recognized, and she had walked up to the podium, looked at the audience, and spoken about her struggles and triumphs as a writer. She had also read briefly from her newly published novel. She hadn't read for very long, but she had read with passion. She had spoken with passion. To me, she had been passion personified.

That afternoon I had purchased only one novel, which had been from the lesser-known author. Perhaps the more famous author hadn't felt a need to win over her audience since her books sell effortlessly whether she does an event or not. On the other hand, maybe she had just been having a bad day. We all do. Most authors, though, have to remember that they need to work in order to sell copies of their book.

Chapter 12

HOW THEY DID IT

I have already introduced you to some authors in previous chapters, but this is an ideal time to share some examples of what many of them did right in doing events for their books. As you're reading, let me remind you to consider some of these ideas for your own book events. After all, imitation is a form of flattery for those who have already blazed the trail.

Another author I interviewed for this book is Susanne Severeid, who wrote a murder mystery titled *The Death of Milly Mahoney* (iUniverse). When I asked Susanne what type of events she had done so far for her novel, she said she did both major and independent bookstores. Once word began to spread, she had then been asked by the main library in her town to give a talk about self-publishing. Since Susanne has acted professionally, talking in front of people came to her rather easily. The only issue was that the library's policy did not allow for the sale of books, but the author had been prepared by making sure that press releases were available for her audience, providing information where to purchase the book. However, just as she was building momentum, Susanne had relocated with her family to another state, one where she had no contacts, but the author said she got lucky.

"I happened to meet up with the director of our local theater arts center," she said, "and since my murder mystery is set in Southern California against the backdrop of the entertainment industry and I'm a former actress, they loved the tie-in. They happened to be looking for ways to bring people in the door to promote some of their other projects as well, and they asked me to do a book signing. All thirty books sold out within an hour and a half. It was so successful that they asked me to come back and give my free self-publishing presentation. We had to bring in extra chairs when over seventy people showed up! Again, we sold out of books."

Susanne may have been lucky, but I dare say it was more that she had an entrepreneurial spirit. It was easy to tell that Susanne was passionate about her career, and she wanted to encourage other authors to get creative about promoting their books. She went on to say, "Yes, try to get into the local bookstores, but even more importantly, check out other venues. With a targeted event, you can sell twenty to thirty books within a short period of time."

Susanne advised authors to know exactly what they will be doing and to be well organized with their book events. Will you serve refreshments? Will you be doing a reading? "Also, think about what you will be signing in people's books. Have a few phrases in mind. The more you plan, the more relaxed you will be and the greater your chance for success."

Susanne is definitely on her way to this success: *The Death of Milly Mahoney* was made Reader's Choice and chosen by Independent Publisher Online to be a highlighted title for July and August of 2006. Hard work pays off. To find out more about what this author is up to check out her Web site at <u>www.susannesevereid.com</u>.

CROSS PROMOTION

Remember earlier when I strongly advised you to have your own Web site in support of your book? *samsara moon* author S. H. Post has done just that. Recently, when I went to his site to see what he was up to, I noticed that he was going to be doing a joint event with artist Kerri McKay. I contacted him and asked how that had come to be. Post said that he had sought McKay out after he had discovered that she had painted some Irish landscapes. Since his novel, in part, takes place in Ireland, both he and McKay decided to do an event together. The event is listed on both Post's and McKay's Web sites, giving it more of an advantage in getting the word out.

But won't the artist eclipse the author or vice versa, you ask? Not at all. As a matter of fact, I have been a panelist with other writers, and a grouping tends to create a buzz. As a collective group, we each brought in a number of people who formulated a small crowd. Not only that, but if every author had the event listed on his or her Web site, imagine how the word could spread. Also, if you are in a writers group, why not ask some of the unpublished authors if they would be interested in sharing a reading with you? Many of these authors are eager to read their writings for an audience and will invite friends and family to come. You will be helping young writers as well as adding to the ripple effect. So try to get to know other authors and see about doing joint events. It is advantageous for everyone.

Take Advantage of All Resources

Rick Spier, novelist of *O'Sullivan's Odyssey* (Moon Donkey Press, LLC), is another author who has found a unique way to promote his events. I met Rick Spier at BookExpo in Washington DC and soon discovered he's been busy. Spier was a finalist for *Foreword* magazine's Book of the Year and PMA Benjamin Franklin Awards, first runner-up for Writers Notes Book Awards, and a semifinalist for Independent Publisher IPPY Awards.

But what has contributed to his success? First, all of his mailings include the phone number and Web site where he is doing his events, for those who might want to purchase a copy of the book but cannot attend. Second, for each event, Spier hosts a reception before the reading, which includes live music by an uilleann piper (Irish bagpipes) and an hors d'oeuvres spread with Irish cheeses, butter, smoked salmon, soda bread baked by the author himself, and a selection of wines. Spier did not choose these particular food items randomly but because they complemented his novel's theme.

But that is not where it ends for this author. He held an event in cooperation with his local Irish heritage club and Irish import shop, each of whom publish a newsletter where he advertises his events. Dartmouth College is the author's alma mater, and, when Spier did an event at the Dartmouth bookstore, he did a direct mailing to all of his classmates, professors, and staff in departments he felt would be interested in the book, including history, creative writing, and English, as well as to the college librarians.

Spier also took advantage of his wife's business and her extensive mailing list. For the events that he did, he invited his wife's clients, including a personalized note from her, to all who lived in the area where he was doing the event.

Finally, because Spier lived in the same neighborhood as the Margaret Mitchell House and Museum in Atlanta, as well as his distant relation to the *Gone With the Wind* author, he found a way to hold an event there. Imagine doing an event where Margaret Mitchell once lived! That must have been such a thrill. Spier gave high school classmates, as well as members from local Irish-interest clubs, the opportunity to share in that thrill by sending them an announcement, inviting them to attend.

Spier felt that an author must do everything he can to promote an event in order for it to be well attended. One unique way that Spier promotes his events is by looking up all the "O'Sullivans" and "Sullivans" in the phone book and personally inviting them to his event. How ingenious! It is this type of creativity that will get you an audience—and perhaps even some press.

Not everyone, though, has a book titled with a surname and will need to find their own unique way to build excitement so they will come! Hopefully, by now you have been brainstorming with your own creative ideas.

A Hair Salon?

When *Without Grace* was about to be released, the staff at Tracy Spinelli's hair salon, Hair Effex, could not have been more excited for me. I'd been patronizing Tracy's salon ever since it first opened. I invited the staff to my book launch in Manhattan, and many of the women came for it, but then Tracy and marketing director Doretta Raffio decided that they, too, wanted to give me a party. Although one wouldn't normally find books for sale in a hair salon, Doretta thought that the marketing could also be used to inform customers that the salon was going to be open on Sundays, which was something new. Even if part of the intention was to get the word out that the salon was beginning Sunday hours, I was thrilled to be instrumental in helping in that effort. For weeks prior, amid hair products, the salon had my book on display with a sign announcing the upcoming event and new Sunday hours. Clients who came in for cuts and highlights began buying copies of my novel. As an aside, I also listed the event on my Web site.

The day of the party, clients showed up to have me sign their books. Other customers who had heard about the event came by out of curiosity. The party was lighthearted and fun, but, once it was over, Doretta decided she wanted to do something more. Every author should have a Doretta in their life! She invited all the customers who had read the book to come back on another Sunday afternoon a couple of months later for a book discussion, with me joining in.

For both events, Doretta included information and a photo of my novel in the Hair Effex newsletter. This is a busy salon, and that was unpaid advertising working to my advantage.

I strongly suggest that you look for the same kind of advantages for your book. A plethora of clubs would quite likely be happy to have a published author as a guest. From Kiwanis Clubs to church organizations, there is a market to be tapped. What about your gym? Even though an event would not work at the gym where I workout by any stretch of the imagination, I asked if I could donate a copy of my book and have it on display at the front desk. I pasted information about where the book could be purchased and was grateful that I was given permission to do so. To my delight, there were occasions when I walked in to find one of the personnel staffing the desk deep into the pages of my novel. (Again, that is the best unpaid advertising one can have!) Not much later, some of the staff members were buying their own copies.

Perhaps you have a platform that would complement the ambience of a gym. Is your book health-related or health food oriented? Find out what is the slowest time for the gym and see if you can book an event for then. Any gym would be happy to draw attention to its services, and you would be bringing in possible new clients—maybe even some media if you pitched it right.

Doretta Raffio, marketing director at Hair Effex.

My book signing
at Hair Effex.

Good friend Peggy Zieran,
offering support.

Chapter 13

RIPPLE EFFECT

Earlier, I shared with you the events that Gerard F. Bianco, author of *The Deal Master,* had been doing. Not too long ago, I received the following e-mail from him:

> At this stage of my promoting, I've reached many of the goals I set for myself when I first began. I've decided that now it's time to regroup and see in which direction I'd like to continue. First stages of promoting are easily identified. It's when you reach the stage that I'm in now that things are not as clear. You have to be more subtle and exact. It's like visiting a city for the first time, you go to all the important monuments, and sights-a no-brainer. It's when you come back a second and third time you're able to explore the more subtle aspects of the city.

As a published author, you will get to this point as well, but don't be discouraged, since you will find ways to create that ripple effect. This chapter will provide some suggestions for you and Bianco to consider.

USE THE INTERNET

Do you remember earlier when publicist Gene Taft said that authors have to hustle to get an audience? Well, Taft also acknowledges that the author tour is changing, since the world is now connected via the Internet. This means that more and more authors are doing podcasts. This not only saves money and time on author tour expenses, but it also reaches a larger audience. Another advantage is that these programs are often archived.

Some time ago, after contacting Antoinette Kuritz, host of Writer's Roundtable on World Talk Radio, I was invited to be on her show. Each week on Writer's Roundtable, Antoinette Kuritz, along with a variety of cohosts, talk with successful writers, agents, editors, book designers, ghostwriters, reviewers, and others from the writing community. The program airs worldwide. If an author wants to promote his or her book, there is access to do it from home wearing pajamas and sipping coffee. However, remember to maintain an air of professionalism so that it sounds as though you are dressed and at a podium. This very idea should inspire every writer. No longer is your book's success dependent on a time-consuming, expensive tour. That is not to say you shouldn't tour for your book, but there are options if you cannot.

Speaking of the Internet, remember to keep your Web site updated. If people find that you aren't adding new and interesting information, they will be less likely to go to it. Remember, even if you don't have a lot of money to have a Web site that is state of the art in appearance, at least have it include the image of your book, any blurbs you have acquired, and a description and a listing of the events you will be doing.

BRING IT TO THE STAGE!

Earlier, I wrote about Susanne Severeid and the event she did at a local theater arts center. At her event, Severeid hadn't read from her novel but had talked about the process of publishing. Let me suggest another possibility, which is to see if a theater company has actors who would be interested in doing a reading from your book. If you have a novel with powerful dialogue, bringing it to life by a reading from up-and-coming actors would help both the performers as well as sales of your book, not to mention perhaps donating a portion of sales to the theater. If it is a struggling theater and you pitch it to the media in an intriguing way, you've managed to gain some more attention for your book.

USE YOUR EXPERTISE

If you have any particular credentials that you can tout, be sure that the media has them available. Reporters and talk show hosts often look for authorities on specific topics, most likely because something in the news inspired the topic. If they had your press kit in their file and saw that you had a book on the topic they want to cover, they may contact you for a sound bite or a quote in their publication. However, do not wait for the reporter to remember that she has your press kit on file. A quick phone call as a reminder may make all the difference, relieving the reporter of having to find an expert and getting the name of your book in the media once again. That same type of flexibility is important to have in order to do an event at the last minute.

FILLING IN

One late Friday afternoon, interviewer Larry Davidson called and asked if I would fill in for an event at Palmer's Vineyard that Sunday. Earlier, I had written about Larry and the author interviews that he does. Apparently, two authors had to postpone the event—one due to a death in the family and the other due to an important meeting that cropped up. Even though it had been too short of a time for me to do any promotion, without hesitation I said, "Book me!"

That Sunday I took the drive out to eastern Long Island to the vineyard, discovering thirty or so people who came to the event expecting to see the scheduled authors. One couple had driven seventy miles. I knew that I had big shoes to fill. I prepared myself for an annoyed audience because they hadn't been expecting me, in addition to having little idea who I was. To Larry's credit, he remembered much of what my novel was about, as well as my background, and, instead of behaving as though I were a replacement, he set the tone with the audience by letting them know that they weren't being cheated by a bait and switch.

We had a delightful conversation, and the audience had a number of questions for me. Even more fantastic, the vendor who brought my books sold out. (Granted, it wasn't a lot of books due to the short turnaround time, but, when an author can say her books sold out, it simply must be said!)

After the event, I told Larry that if he ever got in a jam again to let me know and that I'd be happy to fill in for whoever canceled. Be sure to let interviewers in your market know that you, too, would be happy and capable of filling in whenever they get a last-minute cancellation.

VACATION PLANS

Chances are, after months of doing events you are exhausted and will need a vacation. You have friends and relatives who've been badgering you to visit. Why not take that vacation but fit in a fun event while doing so? Your friends and relatives could help get the word out, and you could have another book launch in their hometown. Make it a reunion but invite the entire town. Throw some burgers on the grill and see if your friends can host it in their backyard. Again, if pitched the right way, the media may want to cover it. And, while you are traveling, why not search out some book clubs in the area? Send them a copy of your book, press kit, and the reading guide that I'd mentioned earlier. It may be enough to get their interest. Many clubs select their books months in advance, so the earlier you contact them the better. If they like your book, they may just switch their reading schedule in order to accommodate hosting you. Also, you can possibly use that vacation as a tax write-off! (However, find out from your accountant first.)

SOMETHING TO BE SAID FOR SERENDIPITY

Serendipity, followed up by staying in contact with one particular book club member, got this Long Island author invited to Savannah, Georgia, for a book club meeting to discuss *Without Grace*. The serendipity part was a matter of being at the right place at the right time with a good friend. We were attending a dinner theater at the Algonquin Hotel in Manhattan. The show was perfect for the intimate location, since it was about Dorothy Parker, Robert Benchley, and Alexander Woolcot, three original Roundtablers. I cannot help but wonder if the spirit of these writers was at work on that fateful day when my friend invited me to attend the show, because that opportune meeting opened a door for this writer.

While waiting for the show to begin, I was showing the sample cover of *Without Grace*, my soon-to-be-released novel, to my friend. With the close proximity of the tables, Judi Painter couldn't help but be curious. Judi, who is from Savannah, was in New York City with her husband, who was on a business trip. Before the show began, we chatted about my upcoming book release. Judi informed me that she was an avid reader and told me that she was in a book club that gave itself the title Babes with Books. She gave me her business card, inviting me to tell her when my novel was published.

The following information is for all the authors out there who are waiting for something to happen with their book: Stop waiting and make it happen!

As I stated earlier, I have a file filled with contacts I've updated over the years, many who invited me to let them know when my book would be published. Therefore, just as I had done with the other contacts, I sent Judi the announcement, and she responded enthusiastically. If I hadn't taken the time to stay in touch with her, chances are she wouldn't have shared the news with her book club and they wouldn't have ordered the book and read it.

Fortunately, they enjoyed *Without Grace* very much and invited me to come to Savannah, Georgia, to participate in the book discussion. Savannah is about a 900-mile drive from my home. The book club went so far as to offer to pay for my flight, but then Peggy, whom I mentioned earlier, suggested we take some time and drive down. I believe adventure makes one a better writer, and so we took a leisurely drive (with the radio blasting) down south. The trip proved successful on many fronts.

Not only was Judi instrumental in getting her club to read my book, but she managed to get reporter Rexanna Lester from *Savannah Morning News* to attend the discussion, which was first preceded by a Southern home-cooked meal. A few days later, there was a generous article, including a photo of me autographing my book, in the newspaper. The article mentioned the title of my novel several times while quoting some of the members' responses. Not only that, but the article informed readers that I contributed to Arianna Huffington's book *On Becoming Fearless,* which would be released in the fall of 2006.

But why would the reporter take her time out of her schedule to attend a book club discussion for an author who is certainly not a household name and not from Savannah? Simple. Judi knew how to pitch the story. She didn't tell Rexanna a whole lot about *Without Grace,* except to say that the club had loved it. What she focused on was how and where she and I had first met: the Algonquin Hotel, a place synonymous with writers of distinction. That, initially, was the story. Here is how much of that original hook was used in the article:[12]

> Painter met Hoenig when they were seated near each other at a dinner theater last summer at the Algonquin Hotel in New York. Hoenig was about to publish "Without Grace" and Painter invited the author to come to Savannah to talk to the book club.

12 Rexanna Lester, "Book Club Finds 'Grace' with New Author," *Savannah Morning News,* April 12, 2006

The rest of the article was mostly about my novel with some discussion being about this warm and wonderful group of women.

Initially, when I was first invited to take the trip to Savannah, there were some who asked me if it was worth my time. Without knowing about the article that would have come from it, I had said yes. When an author wants to build a fan base, he or she should not turn down opportunities—even if they are nine hundred miles away.

There have been at least three other book clubs who have selected my novel of which I'm aware. I only attended one other discussion, and that took place within a short drive from my home. Book clubs are a great venue, and, if you inform them that you would be willing to participate, that may be enough of an enticement to get them to buy and discuss your book. Also, if you create a reading group guide for them with questions based on your book, that will be helpful to the leader of the book club in directing the discussion. Remember, it is all about making it so easy for your contacts that they have no reason to turn you down.

Reporter Rexanna from Savannah taking notes for her column.

Discussing *Without Grace* with my new friends from Savannah, Georgia.

Babes with Books Bookclub in Savannah, Georgia.

Chapter 14

================

A FEW MORE QUICK TIPS

There are many other possibilities to be explored in doing events, and often it simply depends on the book and its topic. However, do not hesitate to return to venues where you have had successful events. Perhaps you could celebrate the first-year anniversary of the publication of your book at these venues.

Speaking Engagements

If you are eager to talk about your book and are confident in doing so, try finding a speaker's bureau for representation. Again, you will need to pitch yourself as a professional and someone who is well versed in your subject matter. There are a number of speakers' bureaus sites on the Internet. Initially, authors must be willing to give talks and not count on making money, but, once the dues have been paid and you have testimonials, it will be easier to find a bureau who will want to represent you.

Finding That Fresh Hook

There are many, many organizations that have a day, week, or month set aside as an acknowledgment or reason to celebrate. As I suggested earlier, *Chase's Calendar of Events: The Day to Day Directory to Special Days,*

Weeks and Months is packed with information that any author would be interested in having. I'm going to list a few for each month below and ask that you consider ways that you may use it as your hook. Don't stretch it, but if it makes sense, implement it!

January: Martin Luther King's Birthday

- January is Eye Care Month
- January is National Hobby Month
- January is National Soup Month
- January is National Staying Healthy Month
- January is National Thank You Month
- January is Oatmeal Month

February: Valentine's Day

- February is American Heart Month
- February is American History Month
- February is Black History Month
- February is Children's Dental Health Month
- February is International Friendship Month
- February is National Cherry Month
- February is National Embroidery Month
- February is National Grapefruit Month
- February is National Snack Food Month
- February is National Wild Bird Feeding Month
- February is Responsible Pet Owners' Month

March:

- March is American Red Cross Month
- March is Music in Our Schools Month
- March is National Craft Month
- March is National Frozen Food Month
- March is National Noodle Month
- March is National Nutrition Month
- March is Women's History Month
- March is Youth Art Month
- March is Independent Publisher Month

April:

- April is Autism Awareness Month
- April is International Guitar Month
- April is Keep America Beautiful Month
- April is National Child Abuse Prevention Month
- April is National Frog Month
- April is National Garden Month
- April is National Humor Month
- April is National Mathematics Education Month
- April is National Poetry Month
- April is Stress Awareness Month

May:

- May is Leave a Legacy Month
- May is Bicycle Safely Month

June:

- June is Dairy Month
- June is National Adopt-A-Cat Month
- June is National Drive Safe Month
- June is National Fresh Fruit and Vegetable Month
- June is National Iced Tea Month
- June is National Rose Month
- June is National Safety Month
- June is National Tennis Month
- June is Turkey Lovers Month
- June is Zoo and Aquarium Month

July:

- July is Anti-Boredom Month
- July is National Baked Bean Month
- July is National Blueberry Month
- July is National Hot Dog Month
- July is National Ice Cream Month
- July is National Picnic Month
- July is National Recreation Month

August:

- August is American Artist Appreciation Month
- August is Foot Health Month
- August is Home Business Month
- August is National Catfish Month
- August is National Golf Month
- August is National Inventors Month
- August is National Water Quality Month

September:

- September is Baby Safety Month
- September is Better Breakfast Month
- September is Cable TV Month
- September is Children's Eye Health and Safety Month
- September is Classical Music Month
- September is Library Card Sign-Up Month
- September is National Chicken Month
- September is National Courtesy Month
- September is National Honey Month
- September is National Pediculosis Prevention Month
- September is National Piano Month
- September is National Rice Month
- September is National School Success Month

- September is National Sewing Month
- September is Read-A-New-Book Month
- September is Women of Achievement Month

October:

- October is Adopt-a-Shelter-Animal Month
- October is Computer Learning Month
- October is Family History Month
- October is National Apple Month
- October is National Clock Month
- October is National Dessert Month
- October is National Pizza Month
- October is National Popcorn Popping Month
- October is National Roller Skating Month
- October is Polish American History Month
- October is National Stamp Collecting Month

November:

- November is Aviation Month
- November is Child Safety and Protection Month
- November is Good Nutrition Month
- November is International Drum Month
- November is Latin American Month
- November is National Adoption Month

- November is National Epilepsy Month
- November is National Model Railroad Month
- November is Peanut Butter Lovers' Month

December:

- December is Hi Neighbor Month
- December is National Stress Free Family Holiday Month
- December is Safe Toy and Gift Month
- December is Universal Human Rights Month
- December is Write to a Friend Month

Did you see any dates in the list that you could use as your hook? I certainly know that I did. For instance, Library Card Sign-Up Month could be a great way to get the library to host you, if you let them know that you plan to help them bring in people to sign up for a library card. Hosting a "Hi Neighbor" event in December with light refreshments possibly at the town hall while inviting everyone to meet the local celebrity author (you) could be a fun event. If you wrote a book about food and cooking, there are a number of possible hooks that you could use from the list. The possibilities are endless.

I hope that, by now, you have a notepad filled with ideas on how to plan events for your book, as well as the passion to make them happen. Remember, you didn't write a book to let it sit on the shelf. You want people to read it, but it needs to get into their hands. Therefore, if there is one bit of advice I can impress upon you, it would be that it is going to be up to *you* to do so.

Most importantly, congratulations on having written a book. Now go sell it!

AFTERWORD

Over the summer, I attended the christening of my neighbor's baby. Family and friends filled the backyard in celebration of the birth of this precious newborn girl. Just before the cake was sliced, the mom and dad took a few moments to thank everyone for sharing in their joy and said how much they were looking forward to watching their daughter grow.

I couldn't help compare this very real birth with the publication of a book.

A book is an inanimate object, to be sure, but, when it is a book that you have spent hours upon hours writing, editing, and bringing to publication, it is like your baby. Just as my neighbors invited everyone to witness what they brought into the world, you should want to invite everyone to see what you, too, have accomplished. And just like my neighbors who will be helping their daughter learn to walk on her own, you too are giving your book legs by doing successful events.

So take time to celebrate and remember that your book is like your child, and, if nurtured, it will grow to success.

I'd love to hear about it! E-mail me to let me know about the unique events you've done for your book at <u>carolhoenig@carolhoenig.com</u>.

As an events coordinator, I have had the opportunity to work with some notable authors and musicians. I pulled some photos from my personal collection to share with you.

Tony Bennett—A Class Act.

One of my earlier events with Senator Alfonse D'Amato.

Always on—Tracy Ulmann.

"And That's the Way It Is" with Walter Cronkite.

Pulitzer Prize winner—Frank McCourt.

Richard Marx—A man who cares about the Arts.

Kenny Loggins—Taking a break to strike a pose.

Alan King—A legend who will be missed.

Don Knotts—No fumbling sheriff from Mayberry here!

Peggy and I hanging with Graham Nash.

I still have the flowers Kurt Vonnegut pulled from his sleeve and presented to me!

INDEX

978-1-58348-476-0
1-58348-476-0

Printed in the United States
86146LV00004B/253/A

9 781583 484760